# READING WISE 3

## Learning Through Asian Folktales

Helen Kirkpatrick

Compass Publishing

# Contents

## READING WISE 3
**Learning Through Asian Folktales**

Helen Kirkpatrick

© 2011 Compass Publishing

ISBN: 978-1-59966-534-4

10 9 8 7 6 5 4 3 2
15 14 13 12

Acquisitions Editor: Jeremy Monroe
Illustrator: Hieram Weintraub, Lin Wang
Cover/Interior Design: Design Plus

E-mail: info@compasspub.com
http://www.compasspub.com

**Photo Credits**
pp. 34 © iStock International, Inc.
pp. 11, 16, 17, 23, 28, 29, 35, 41, 46, 47, 52, 53, 58, 59, 64, 65, 70, 71, 76, 77, 82, 83, 88, 89, 94, 95, 100, 101, 106, 107, 112, 113, 118, 119, 124, 125, 130 © Shutterstock, Inc.

# How to Teach This Book

*Reading Wise* is a reading series for high beginner and intermediate learners. The book consists of twenty units, each containing ten activities based on the main story of the unit. In particular, each unit includes a short story, a picture-based summary activity, a dialog based on the story for listening and speaking practice, and expansion activities. Expansion activities encourage students' creative use of language by allowing them to express their own opinions and ideas.

## Pre-Reading (5 min.)

The teacher should write the title of the unit on the board. Students should find a partner and look at the picture. Single partners are suggested for this activity so that students can help each other communicate without being nervous in front of the entire class.

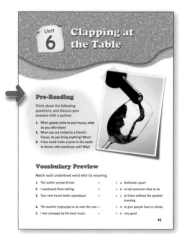

Next, the teacher should go over the questions to make sure the students understand them. Pairs should then ask each other the questions and answer them. Students need NOT come to any consensus on the answers as the questions are designed to activate the students' background knowledge related to the topic. If time allows, have some of the pairs share answers to specific questions. Record useful related vocabulary on the board and discuss how the vocabulary may be related to the reading.

# Vocabulary Preview (10 min.)

In this activity, simple sentences give context to key vocabulary that can be found in the story. It is important that students fully understand each vocabulary word or phrase. This section will give them synonyms to use, which will increase the depth of their language use.

Have students work individually to complete the exercise. They will match the underlined word to its meaning. When they are finished, have students check their answers with their partner. Review the answers as a class. While going through the list of words, ask the class to generate synonyms or antonyms that come to mind for each word. Having the class generate new example sentences using the words will also reinforce the learning of new vocabulary items for students.

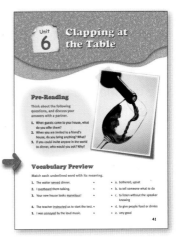

# Reading Passage (5 min.)

Students should read the passages silently for a few minutes. Ask students to underline any words they do not understand while they are reading. If there are, explain what the words mean.

Next, have students complete the "Understanding the Key Ideas" section. They should check their answers with a partner. If they do not agree, refer students to the reading passage again. They can circle the part that indicates the correct answer. This section is meant to be a general review of the story.

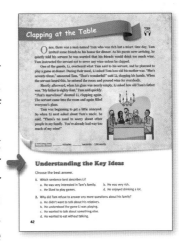

# Reading Comprehension (5 min.)

This section gives teachers an opportunity to see if their students fully understand the passage. If they do not understand specific sections of the reading, the teacher should review difficult portions of the text. Again, students should work alone to complete the questions and then work with a partner to check their answers.

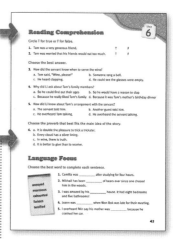

Students should refer to specific places in the story to explain how they reached their answers if these words are too close together. Pointing this out to students makes them responsible for their own understanding and also helps them learn to skim material for information, which is an important skill in reading. It would also be helpful for students to draw a box around portions of the text that show the answers.

# Language Focus (5 min.)

This section consists of various activities that practice grammatical structure. The main purpose of this book is not to teach grammar, though it is important to point out key grammatical aspects while focusing on reading comprehension. Each unit has a different grammar point that the "Language Focus" section covers, and teachers are encouraged to think of ways to make grammar points relevant and interesting. For example, if the section is about adjectives, the teacher can have students brainstorm about different adjectives, creating word bubbles around each word, and linking them to other synonyms.

# Picture Story (5 min.)

Each unit has a picture-story activity that allows students to retell the story in their own words with a bit of guidance. It would be best to have the students work with a partner to encourage them to talk about the story.

First, have students put the story in order, based on the pictures. Students may need to refer to the story to complete the exercise.

Next, have students use the words under each picture to create a full sentence. The words will give them a clue and also provide guidance for actually writing the sentences that explain the story. While answers may vary slightly, the activity is structured so that students will have a lot of support in writing their sentences. As time allows, have volunteers write their sentences on the board to check.

# Act Out the Story (5 min.)

Have students read the dialog related to the story. Students can make guesses as to the correct word to fill in each blank. Share the correct answers with the class.

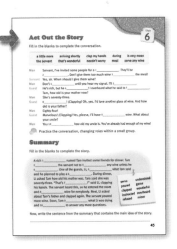

For pronunciation practice, read the dialog aloud. Stop after each phrase of sentence and have students repeat what they heard. A fun variation is to have all the boys repeat the male parts and all the girls repeat the female parts, or split the class in half and have one side repeat one character and the other side repeat the second character. After this practice, students can work in pairs or small groups to recite the dialog together.

If there is time, choose 2-4 pairs to preform the dialog. Seeing the story in live motion will make it more dynamic for students to connect the reading to actual events. The more dynamic the acting, the more likely students will be to remember key elements of the story.

# Summary (5 min.)

By the time students arrive at the summary section, they have already reviewed the story in three different ways: Reading Comprehension, Picture Story, and Act Out the Story. The Summary activity reinforces acquisition of the unit's target vocabulary.

Students should complete the summary section on their own. After they complete the section, the teacher can choose students to read the sentences for the rest of the class, which allows them the opportunity to listen to the summary again, while also checking their answers.

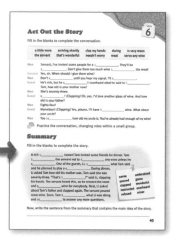

# Expansion Questions (5 min.)

This section is meant to provide students with an opportunity to expand on the lesson in a creative way. These exercises should be completed in small groups to encourage conversation. The teacher should place students into groups of 3-5. For most questions, the answers may vary among students. Therefore, it would be best for teachers to monitor their students' conversations.

Expansion Questions may ask students to share experiences, knowledge, or opinions related in some way to the unit theme. Once everyone has expressed their opinion, the group can choose one person to summarize their discussion for the entire class.

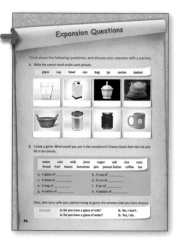

# Supplemental Vocabulary Study

Another component that could help students acquire new vocabulary items would be to create a vocabulary log that students are responsible for and must keep throughout the entire course. Once the teacher reviews the words, students can keep a separate sheet with all of the vocabulary words listed on the left side. Next, students would write the definition of the word. The teacher and students could then create an entirely new sentence, using the word in context. The process of writing and creating a new contextual sentence that has meaning for the student may make the word and definition easier to remember.

| Vocabulary word | Definition |
|---|---|
| Part of speech | New sentence in context |
| (Example) | |
| Feathers | Light, hair-like structures |
| noun | Peacocks have beautiful and colorful feathers. |

# Unit 1

# The Proud Driver

## Pre-Reading

**Think about the following questions, and discuss your answers with a partner.**

1. Do big people and small people behave differently?
2. Do people with important jobs behave differently from those in other jobs? In what ways?
3. Should these people's behavior be different? Why or why not?

## Vocabulary Preview

**Match each underlined word with its meaning.**

1. A <u>carriage</u> was the main form of transportation before cars.

2. Kit <u>noticed</u> that her handbag was open.

3. Joe was <u>amazed</u> at how big the elephant was.

4. Li was <u>shocked</u> when he saw the huge snake.

5. The boy's father was angry because he did not <u>behave</u>.

   a. a vehicle pulled by horses

   b. very surprised

   c. scared

   d. to see or pay attention to

   e. to do things in a polite and correct way

# The Proud Driver

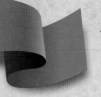 

Once, there was a big man called Yan. He got a job as a driver for the king. The king was a small man and was always polite. Although he was the most important man in the country, he never boasted.

One day, the king asked Yan to take him out in his carriage. The driver sat proudly at the front, shouting at the four horses to go faster. He yelled at people to get out of his way and felt very pleased with himself.

When he returned home that evening, his wife was upset. She said she was going to leave him. Yan was amazed and asked why. She explained, "The king is a very important man, but he isn't proud. He's always quiet and gentle. But you! You're a very big man, but you shout at the horses and you're rude to people. You think you're as important as the king, but you're only his driver. That's why I have decided to leave."

The driver was so shocked that from then on, he started to behave better. The king noticed this change and made Yan his lead driver. Yan's wife was happy with the change and stayed on with him.

Reading Time _____ minutes _____ seconds   204 words

# Understanding the Key Ideas

**Choose the best answer.**

1. What is the story about?
   a. A king being polite
   b. A wife wanting to leave her husband
   c. Making someone behave better
   d. Driving a carriage

2. Why did Yan change the way he behaved?
   a. The king told him to change.
   b. His wife told him to leave.
   c. The king made him his chief driver.
   d. His wife said she was leaving him.

# Reading Comprehension

**Circle T for true or F for false.**

1. At first, Yan thought he was as important as the king.          T          F
2. Yan's wife left him to teach him a lesson.          T          F

**Choose the best answer.**

3. Who was the most important man in the country?
   a. Yan
   b. The king
   c. Yan's wife
   d. The lead driver

4. Why was Yan's wife upset?
   a. She wanted Yan to be the king.
   b. She wanted Yan to be the lead driver.
   c. She wanted Yan to act more like the king.
   d. She wanted Yan to make more money.

5. Why did the king make Yan his lead driver?
   a. Yan begged for the job.
   b. The king noticed Yan's wife.
   c. Yan's wife asked the governor for help.
   d. The king noticed Yan's new attitude.

**Choose the proverb that best fits the main idea of the story.**

6. a. A closed mouth catches no flies.
   b. Don't put the cart before the horse.
   c. A jack of all trades is a master of none.
   d. It takes one to know one.

# Language Focus

**Choose the best preposition to complete each sentence.**

at
about
for
in
of
with

1. Xu has always been afraid _____ the dark.

2. The children were very excited _____ their new dog.

3. Pat is very interested _____ sports.

4. France has always been famous _____ its good food.

5. Ella was delighted _____ her lovely birthday present.

6. Dan was amazed _____ how quickly Jen learned to speak Chinese.

# Picture Story

**A** Number the pictures in the correct order according to the story. Then, talk about each picture.

Yan / going to leave / wife / home

king noticed / lead driver / behaving better

rude to people / shouted at horses / wife said

quiet and gentle / important / wasn't proud

**B** What did you say? Write about each picture using the given words and phrases.

1. _____

2. _____

3. _____

4. _____

14

# Act Out the Story

**Fill in the blanks to complete the conversation.**

| promise | a big | am going to | behave badly | behave better |
| drove the carriage | leave | lead driver | very important | notices |

Driver     *(Loudly)* What a good day I had today! I 1_____ so well!

Wife     *(Quietly)* Oh, did you? Well, I saw and heard you today, and I didn't like what I saw.
So I've decided something. I 2_____ leave you.

Driver     *(In amazement)* 3_____ me? Why?

Wife     Well, the king is not very tall, but he is a 4_____ man. However, he's
always humble and kind. He is also sensitive and 5_____ everything.

Driver     So?

Wife     You may be 6_____ man, but you're always so proud of yourself and
7_____ around everyone. You're only a carriage driver! So I'm going away.

Driver     I'm very sorry. I 8_____ I won't behave like that again.

Wife     If you promise to 9_____, then I won't leave you.

Driver     *(Days later)* Do you know? I have just become the king's 10_____!

Wife     Good! Then I'll stay.

**Practice the conversation, changing roles with a partner.**

# Summary

**Fill in the blanks to complete the story.**

The king was 1_____. His driver, Yan, was
2_____. He always shouted at the horses
3_____. When he 4_____ one night, his
wife told him that she 5_____. Yan
6_____ this. His wife explained that he was not
7_____ the king. He was only a driver, but he
behaved as if he were the most 8_____ in the country.
Yan changed his attitude. When the king saw how different his
9_____, he asked him to become his
10_____. His wife decided not to leave him after all.

lead driver
a small man
attitude was
a big man
important man
to go faster
as important as
returned home
was amazed to hear
was leaving him

**Now, write the sentence from the summary that contains the main idea of the story.**

_____

# Expansion Questions

Work with a partner. Choose one of the photos. Your partner will ask *yes/no* questions until he or she can guess your photo.

| Example | Q: Are people sitting in the carriage? | A: No. |
| | Q: Is the carriage black? | A: Yes. |

# An Expensive Head

## Pre-Reading

**Think about the following questions, and discuss your answers with a partner.**

1. How did people travel before cars, trains, and airplanes? Name three ways.
2. How do people use horses today?
3. How far do you think a horse can run in one day?

## Vocabulary Preview

**Match each underlined word with its meaning.**

1. Please be <u>patient</u> and wait your turn. •
2. The new soccer stadium is <u>enormous</u>! •
3. We left <u>immediately</u> after the movie was over. •
4. I was <u>delighted</u> that you called me. •
5. My teacher was <u>furious</u> at me for fighting at school. •

- • a. very happy
- • b. very angry
- • c. right away
- • d. able to wait
- • e. very large

Track
02

Once, there was a king who owned many kinds of animals, but he did not have a great horse. So he commanded his servants to go and find the fastest horse in the land. They searched for months, but they returned without success.

One day, a servant named Zan heard about a very fast horse in another country. He asked for permission to travel there, and the king agreed. Sadly, when he arrived, he learned that the horse had died. But Zan had an idea. He bought the horse's head for five hundred pieces of silver.

When Zan returned, the king was furious. "You paid five hundred pieces of silver for this?" the king shouted. "What good is it to me? I want a living horse, you fool!"

"Please be patient, my king," the servant said. "When people hear how much you paid for the head of a dead horse, they will think you will pay an enormous amount for a living one! People from around the world will bring their horses to you!"

That's just what happened. Almost immediately, people all over the world started bringing their fast horses. The king was delighted, and he soon found exactly the horse he wanted.

**Reading Time** _____ minutes _____ seconds   201 words

# Understanding the Key Ideas

**Choose the best answer.**

1. What is the story about?
   a. A clever servant
   b. An unsuccessful king
   c. A dead horse
   d. A horse race

2. What was Zan's plan?
   a. To make the king very angry
   b. To spend the king's money
   c. To travel the world looking for horses
   d. To get many people to bring their horses to the king

# Reading Comprehension

**Circle T for true or F for false.**

1. The king had many kinds of animals.　　　T　　　F
2. The king's servants brought many horses to him.　　T　　　F

**Choose the best answer.**

3. What did Zan discover about the fast horse when he arrived?
    a. It was not really fast at all.
    b. It was not alive.
    c. It was not for sale.
    d. Someone had already bought it.

4. How did the king feel when Zan returned?
    a. He was delighted.
    b. He was frightened.
    c. He was furious.
    d. He was sad.

5. Why did people bring horses to the king?
    a. The servant bought the horses.
    b. They wanted to give them as gifts.
    c. They expected a lot of money.
    d. The king commanded them.

**Choose the proverb that best fits the main idea of the story.**

6. a. You can lead a horse to water, but you can't make him drink.
    b. Money makes the world go around.
    c. You're beating a dead horse.
    d. Every cloud has a silver lining.

# Language Focus

**Choose the best word or phrase to complete each sentence.**

would buy

had bought

bought

buy

will buy

1. Every day I go to the store and _____ bread.

2. If I had a million dollars, I _____ an airplane.

3. When Kim opened the bag, she realized that she _____ the wrong book.

4. I _____ some flowers for my mother's birthday tomorrow.

5. Two days ago, I _____ ten apples and they are already gone.

# Picture Story

**A** Number the pictures in the correct order according to the story. Then, talk about each picture.

three years / horse /
found / king liked

delighted / find /
exactly horse / wanted

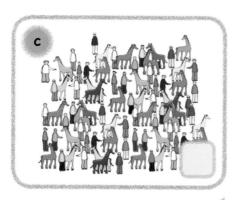

soon / people began /
horses / king to see

furious / wanted fastest horse /
world / not / expensive, dead

**B** What did you say? Write about each picture using the given words and phrases.

1. _____
2. _____
3. _____
4. _____

# Act Out the Story

**Fill in the blanks to complete the conversation.**

| be patient | exactly what | have permission | in the world | enormous |
| just one problem | larger amount | pieces of silver | was once | living |

**King**     Nobody has found the fastest horse 1_____.

**Servant**  Sir, may I 2_____ to go and look for the horse that you want?

**King**     Yes, you may.

**Man**      *(Later)* I have a wonderful horse! It 3_____ very fast! But there is

4_____. My horse died last week.

**Servant**  It's OK. But I only want the horse's head. Here are five hundred 5_____.

**King**     *(Later, angrily)* That's an 6_____ amount of money for a dead horse!

I want a horse that is still 7_____!

**Servant**  Sir, please 8_____! If people know what you paid for a dead horse,

they'll think you will pay a 9_____ for a living one.

**King**     *(A week later)* I have found 10_____ I want!

**Practice the conversation, changing roles within a small group.**

# Summary

**Fill in the blanks to complete the story.**

A king 1_____ his servants to find the 2_____ horse in the
world. They searched for months without 3_____. A servant named Zan
heard about a very fast horse in another country. When he 4_____, he
learned that the horse was dead. But he bought the horse's head for
five hundred pieces of 5_____. When Zan
returned, the king was 6_____. But the servant
explained that now people would believe that the king
would pay an 7_____ amount for a living horse.
Almost 8_____, people from all around the
world started 9_____ their fast horses. The king
soon found 10_____ the horse he wanted
because of the actions of his servant.

| exactly | enormous |
| silver | furious |
| success | fastest |
| immediately | arrived |
| commanded | bringing |

**Now, write the sentence from the summary that contains the main idea of the story.**

_____

# Expansion Questions

**Imagine that a rich uncle has died and left a million dollars for you.**

1. What would you buy for yourself?

   _____

2. What would you buy for your family?

   _____

3. What would you buy for your friends?

   _____

**Imagine that your rich uncle's will specifies that you have to give away half of the money to help others. Who would you give the money to? How would it help those people? Name three ways.**

| Example | I would help feed hungry people in Africa. |
| --- | --- |

_____

_____

_____

# Unit 3

# The Sparrow with No Tail

## Pre-Reading

**Think about the following questions, and discuss your answers with a partner.**

1. What kinds of birds live near you?
2. What do birds eat?
3. Do birds like living near people? Why or why not?

## Vocabulary Preview

**Match each underlined word with its meaning.**

1. The farmer <u>plucked</u> a feather from the bird. •
2. I <u>rushed</u> home quickly. •
3. She <u>offered</u> us something to eat. •
4. The <u>elderly</u> man had five grandchildren. •
5. The thief stole the <u>jewels</u>. •

• a. old
• b. beautiful, expensive stones
• c. to pull out
• d. to go fast
• e. to give

# The Sparrow with No Tail

One day, a greedy woman was drying rice outside her house. A sparrow flew down and began to eat some of the rice. The woman was furious and shouted, "You thief!" She caught the sparrow and pulled out his tail feathers. "That will teach you to steal from me!"

A kind elderly couple lived next door. They saw what happened and followed the sparrow to his nest in the plum tree. The sparrow was delighted to see them and invited them to meet his wife. The couple gave the sparrows a bowl of rice. Then, the sparrow's wife brought two baskets, one heavy, one light. She asked them to choose one to take home. The couple wasn't greedy, so they chose the lighter basket. They were amazed to find the basket full of gold and jewels.

When the greedy woman heard about this, she rushed to the plum tree. The sparrow's wife offered her a choice between the two baskets. She chose the heavier one. As soon as she arrived home, she opened it. But instead of gold and jewels, the basket was full of angry birds. They flew around her head and plucked out her hair!

**Reading Time** _____ minutes _____ seconds   192 words

# Understanding the Key Ideas

**Choose the best answer.**

1. What is the story about?
   a. How to dry rice
   b. What happens to unkind people
   c. Where to find a sparrow's house
   d. How to keep a thief from stealing

2. What could be another title for the story?
   a. Feeding Birds
   b. A Reward for Greed
   c. Catching a Thief
   d. Gold and Jewels

# Reading Comprehension

**Circle T for true or F for false.**

1. The woman didn't mind sharing her rice.             T          F
2. The elderly couple was rewarded for their kindness.    T          F

**Choose the best answer.**

3. What did the woman do to the sparrow?
   a. She put him in a small basket.          b. She threw rice at him.
   c. She pulled out his tail feathers.       d. She pulled his nest from the tree.

4. Why did the elderly couple go to the plum tree?
   a. To look for gold and jewels           b. To show kindness to the sparrow
   c. To pick some plums to eat             d. To give the sparrow a basket

5. Why did the woman take the heavy basket?
   a. She liked the color better.           b. She wanted more gold and jewels.
   c. She was very strong.                  d. It was the only basket the sparrow offered.

**Choose the proverb that best fits the main idea of the story.**

6. a. Beggars can't be choosers.           b. A bird in the hand is worth two in the bush.
   c. Birds of a feather flock together.    d. What comes around goes around.

# Language Focus

**Choose the best preposition to complete each sentence.**

at

for

in

on

out

to

1. I need to find _____ when the train leaves.

2. James took us to the cinema and paid _____ our tickets.

3. She put her jewels _____ a secret box to keep them safe from thieves.

4. My first class starts _____ eight, so I need to leave for school by seven.

5. Everyone should go _____ the dentist at least once a year.

6. The teacher is always _____ time and doesn't like students to be late.

# Picture Story

**A** Number the pictures in the correct order according to the story. Then, talk about each picture.

at home / opened basket /
found / full of

when / sparrow's wife offered /
basket / chose / heavier

sparrow ate / rice / so /
pulled out / feathers

sparrow's wife / asked couple /
choose / chose / lighter

**B** What did you say? Write about each picture using the given words and phrases.

1. _____

2. _____

3. _____

4. _____

26

# Act Out the Story

**Fill in the blanks to complete the conversation.**

| beautiful jewels | quite heavy | share a meal | sparrow's tail feathers |
| visit you | that heavy one | the lighter one | treasure | rice | angry birds |

| | |
|---|---|
| Sparrow | I'm hungry, and that looks like food! |
| Woman | I'll stop you from stealing! You won't steal my 1_____ again! |
| Elderly Lady | Did you see? She pulled out the 2_____! Let's go and see if he's okay. *(Later)* Hello, sparrow! We've come to 3_____ and bring you some rice. |
| Sparrow's Wife | Thank you! Would you 4_____ with us? *(Later)* We have two baskets to offer you. Please choose one. |
| Elderly Lady | This basket looks 5_____. So may we have 6_____? *(That night)* Look at all these 7_____! Let's put the 8_____ somewhere safe. Look! The basket is filling up again! |
| Woman | *(The next day)* I want a basket, too. I'll take 9_____! *(At home)* There must be even more treasure in this heavy basket! *(Loud screaming)* Oh no! It's full of 10_____! |

**Practice the conversation, changing roles within a small group.**

# Summary

**Fill in the blanks to complete the story.**

A sparrow ate some rice that 1_____ to a greedy woman. She caught the sparrow and pulled out his 2_____ feathers. A kind elderly couple 3_____ the sparrow to his nest and gave him a 4_____ of rice. The sparrow's wife 5_____ them two baskets – one heavy, one light. The couple took the 6_____ one and found it full of gold and 7_____. When the greedy woman heard about this, she 8_____ to the tree. The sparrow's wife offered her two baskets, too. She chose the 9_____ one. But the basket was full of angry birds that 10_____ out her hair!

| | |
|---|---|
| heavier | offered |
| plucked | rushed |
| jewels | lighter |
| followed | tail |
| bowl | belonged |

**Now, write the sentence from the summary that contains the main idea of the story.**

_____

# Expansion Questions

**Work with a partner to figure out how old each person is and what treasure they have.**

Age: _____
Treasure: _____

Age: _____
Treasure: _____

Age: _____
Treasure: _____

A farmer, a teacher, and a doctor each have one treasure: a gold coin, a silver cup, or a jewel. One person is 34, another is 36, and the third is 38.

The owner of the gold coin is not the youngest.
The farmer, who owns something metal, is 36.
Neither the doctor nor the 38-year-old owns the gold coin.
The owner of the silver cup is two years younger than the farmer.

**Now, fill in the blanks with different clues from those above to create a new quiz. Tell your partner the clues and see if he or she can guess the correct answers.**

Age: _____
Treasure: _____

Age: _____
Treasure: _____

Age: _____
Treasure: _____

The owner of the _____ is not the youngest.
The _____, who owns something metal, is _____.
Neither the _____ nor the _____-year-old owns the gold coin.
The owner of the silver cup is two years _____ (younger/older) than the _____.

# No Strawberries in Winter

## Pre-Reading

Think about the following questions, and discuss your answers with a partner.

1. What is your favorite fruit?
2. Do you like fruit that comes from another country? Name some of these fruits.
3. What fruits grow in spring, summer, or fall?

## Vocabulary Preview

Match each underlined word with its meaning.

1. Aspirin is a <u>cure</u> for headaches. •
2. It is <u>impossible</u> for rocks to speak. •
3. I <u>demanded</u> to see the owner. •
4. We <u>searched</u> for the restaurant but couldn't find it. •
5. She was <u>ashamed</u> of her son's behavior. •

- • a. to look for
- • b. to be embarrassed
- • c. unable to happen
- • d. a treatment to make something better
- • e. to ask for something angrily

# No Strawberries in Winter

Track 04

Once, there was a rich master who was mean to his servants. He would ask them to do impossible things and then punish them when they failed. One winter, he said he felt ill and that the only cure was strawberries. He ordered a servant to find some. "But, sir, that's impossible. It's winter," said the servant. "Bring me strawberries tomorrow!" the master demanded.

The servant was worried as he walked home through the deep snow. He knew that he would fail and be punished. At home, his son heard about the problem, but he told his father not to worry.

Early the next morning, the boy went to the master's house. When he saw the boy, the master demanded his strawberries. The boy apologized that he had no strawberries. He said that his father had searched for them, but he was then bitten by a poisonous snake and was now home in bed.

The master grew angry. "Do you think I'm stupid?" he shouted. "It's winter! It's too cold for snakes!" The boy then asked, "If it's too cold for snakes, why is it not too cold for strawberries?" The master was ashamed and walked away. He never again asked anyone to do something impossible.

**Reading Time** _____ minutes _____ seconds   212 words

# Understanding the Key Ideas

**Choose the best answer.**

**1.** What is the story about?
- a. A boy who changed a cruel man
- b. A boy who had a pet snake
- c. A man who looked for strawberries
- d. A master who was very ill

**2.** Why did the boy tell his father not to worry?
- a. He would find the strawberries for the master.
- b. He knew how to cure the master without strawberries.
- c. He would take the punishment for his father.
- d. He knew how to make the master ashamed of his behavior.

# Reading Comprehension

**Circle T for true or F for false.**

1. The master always asked for impossible things.       T       F
2. The servant did not worry about the master's demand.       T       F

**Choose the best answer.**

3. Why was the master cruel?
    a. He never shared his food with his servants.   b. He made people work in winter.
    c. He enjoyed seeing his servants fail.          d. He had poisonous snakes.

4. Why was the servant worried as he walked home?
    a. He knew he would be punished.                 b. The snow was very deep.
    c. He had no strawberries for his son.           d. He did not have enough money.

5. How do we know that the master was truly ashamed?
    a. He cried and walked away.                     b. He apologized to the boy.
    c. He changed his behavior.                      d. He gave the servant a new job.

**Choose the proverb that best fits the main idea of the story.**

6. a. When it rains, it pours.
    b. Slow and steady wins the race.
    c. You can't squeeze blood from a stone.
    d. A candle loses nothing by lighting another candle.

# Language Focus

**Match the situation on the left with the correct instruction or order on the right.**

1. You are at the doctor to get a shot. •                 • a. Don't worry! It won't hurt much!

2. Your father is telling you to leave   •                • b. Please come in. Make yourself at home.
   for school.

3. You are in a kitchen.                •                 • c. Hurry up! You'll be late.

4. Somebody invites you into their      •                 • d. Turn left after the big green house. It's across the road.
   house.

5. You are near a dirty river.          •                 • e. No swimming!

6. You need to find a post office.      •                 • f. Don't touch the pot. It's hot!

# Picture Story

**A** Number the pictures in the correct order according to the story. Then, talk about each picture.

master ashamed / never asked / something impossible

servant worried / knew fail / punished

asked why / too cold / snakes / not too cold / strawberries

shouted / think stupid / too cold / snakes

**B** What did you say? Write about each picture using the given words and phrases.

1. _____

2. _____

3. _____

4. _____

# Act Out the Story

**Fill in the blanks to complete the conversation.**

| bit him | cure me | tomorrow | don't find | if it's too cold | punish me |
| wrong | searched everywhere | that's impossible | something impossible | | |

Rich Man   Servant, I feel ill! The only thing that will 1_____ is strawberries.

Servant   But it's winter, sir, so 2_____! Strawberries don't grow in winter.

Rich Man   I want strawberries! Bring me some 3_____!

Boy   *(That night)* What's 4_____, Dad? You look worried.

Servant   If I don't get strawberries, my master will 5_____!

Boy   Don't worry, Dad.

Rich Man   *(The next morning)* What do you want, boy?

Boy   My father 6_____ for strawberries. But then a poisonous snake
7_____.

Rich Man   Do you think I'm stupid, boy? It's winter! You 8_____ snakes in winter.

Boy   Sir, 9_____ for snakes, why isn't it too cold for strawberries?

Rich Man   I'm ashamed. I know it's wrong to ask for 10_____.

💬 **Practice the conversation, changing roles within a small group.**

# Summary

**Fill in the blanks to complete the story.**

Once, a mean master 1_____ that his servant find strawberries in winter.
The servant knew that he would 2_____ and be 3_____. At home,
his son heard about the 4_____, but he told his father
not to 5_____. The next morning, the boy told the
master that his father had 6_____ for strawberries,
but he was 7_____ by a poisonous snake and had
to go home. The master said it was too 8_____ for
snakes. The boy said that it must also be too cold for
strawberries. The master was 9_____, and he never
again asked anyone to do something 10_____.

| problem | cold |
| worry | bitten |
| searched | impossible |
| punished | fail |
| demanded | ashamed |

**Now, write the sentence from the summary that contains the main idea of the story.**

_____

# Expansion Questions

**Look at the signs. What do they mean? Work with a partner to finish the sentences.**

1. Please don't _____

2. Be careful, there are _____

3. Watch out for _____

4. Be careful, there are _____

5. Please don't _____

6. Watch out for _____

**Make your own signs, one for your classroom and one for your city. Tell your partner what they mean.**

# Unit 5 Paying Back Money

## Pre-Reading

**Think about the following questions, and discuss your answers with a partner.**

1. Have you asked someone for money? Who was it?
2. Has anyone asked you for money? What do they need it for?
3. Besides money, what other things do people borrow? Name three things.

## Vocabulary Preview

**Match each underlined word or phrase with its meaning.**

1. I studied <u>exceedingly</u> hard for the exam. •
2. Hurry! We're <u>about to</u> leave. •
3. He <u>owes</u> me five dollars. •
4. Talking when someone else is talking is <u>rude</u>. •
5. I need to <u>reduce</u> my weight by 10 kg. •

• a. almost going to happen
• b. more than expected or necessary
• c. to make smaller or less
• d. to need to pay back
• e. not respectful

35

# Paying Back Money

Mr. Wang was a very wealthy and generous man. One day, he invited three men who owed him money to his house. He announced that if they promised to repay him in their next lives, he would reduce the amount they owed by half.

One man said he would come back as a horse so he could work exceedingly hard for Mr. Wang. Mr. Wang agreed and let him go. A second man said he would return as a cow so he could provide plenty of milk. Mr. Wang agreed and dismissed him as well.

The third man, who owed the most, said he would be reborn as Mr. Wang's father. Mr. Wang was furious. This man owed him a lot of money, and yet he was being very rude. Mr. Wang was about to throw him out of his house when the man began to explain. He said, "If I returned as your father, then I could save all my money and buy land and horses to give you. In that way, I could return what I owe and more!" Hearing this, Mr. Wang understood and said, "Your answer has pleased me very much! You owe me nothing!"

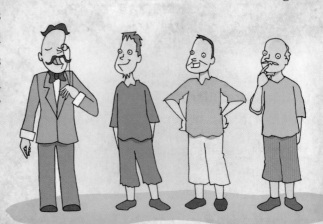

**Reading Time** _____ minutes _____ seconds   199 words

# Understanding the Key Ideas

**Choose the best answer.**

1. Why did Mr. Wang invite the three men?
   a. To get all his money back
   b. To ask them to lend him money
   c. To buy some horses and cows
   d. To give them a generous offer

2. Which man had the most clever answer?
   a. Mr. Wang
   b. The third man
   c. The first man
   d. The second man

# Reading Comprehension

**Circle T for true or F for false.**

1. Mr. Wang owed a lot of money.             T      F

2. Mr. Wang asked the three men to come and work for him.    T      F

**Choose the best answer.**

3. How do we know that Mr. Wang was a generous man?
   a. He often invited people to his house.     b. He gave lots of milk to people.
   c. He offered to reduce what people owed to him.   d. His father told him to be generous.

4. Why was Mr. Wang upset that the third man wanted to return as his father?
   a. The man was much younger than Mr. Wang.    b. It was a rude thing to say.
   c. Mr. Wang did not like his father.            d. Mr. Wang's father was not dead.

5. Why was the third man's answer better than the other men's?
   a. He could repay only what he owed.      b. He could work hard for Mr. Wang.
   c. He could pay back half of the money.     d. He could repay all that he owed and more.

**Choose the proverb that best fits the main idea of the story.**

6. a. Never leave an unsettled debt.           b. Even a broken clock is right twice a day.
   c. Neither a borrower nor a lender be.     d. Like father, like son.

# Language Focus

**Choose the best word or phrase to complete each sentence.**

1. _____ very large.
   a. Elephants is     b. An elephant is     c. An elephant are    d. Elephants

2. I'd like _____.
   a. milks          b. a milk        c. some milk      d. some milks

3. Do you have any _____?
   a. rice           b. rices         c. some rices     d. a rice

4. My uncles are _____.
   a. a farmer       b. the farmer     c. farmer        d. farmers

# Picture Story

**A** Number the pictures in the correct order according to the story. Then, talk about each picture.

a

agreed / told /
two men / could go

b

how dare / be impolite /
about / father

c

owe / thousands / want /
reborn / father

d

save all / money / give /
much more / owe now

**B** What did you say? Write about each picture using the given words and phrases.

1. _____

2. _____

3. _____

4. _____

# Act Out the Story

**Fill in the blanks to complete the conversation.**

| don't hit me | lent | I can save | I have lent you | cow | I'd like to |
|---|---|---|---|---|---|
| much more from me | owe me | to be reborn | to pay me back | | |

| | |
|---|---|
| Mr. Wang | I've 1_____ money to all of you. If you promise 2_____ in the next life, I'll forget about the money 3_____ already. |
| First Man | I hope 4_____ as a horse. Then, I can work for you. |
| Mr. Wang | Agreed! You can go now. |
| Second Man | If I come back as a 5_____, I can give you plenty of milk. |
| Mr. Wang | Yes, that's good. You also can go now. |
| Third Man | 6_____ come back as your father. |
| Mr. Wang | You 7_____ a lot, yet you are being very rude about my father. |
| Third Man | Please 8_____! I'll explain. If I'm your father, 9_____ all my money. In that way, you will get 10_____ than I owe you now. |
| Mr. Wang | Oh, now I understand. That's a great idea! You, too, can go now! |

💬 **Practice the conversation, changing roles within a small group.**

# Summary

**Fill in the blanks to complete the story.**

Three men 1_____ money to Mr. Wang. He announced that if they 2_____ him in their next lives, he would 3_____ the amount they owed by half. One man said he would come back as a 4_____ and work hard for Mr. Wang. A second man said he would return as a cow and give Mr. Wang milk. The third man said he would be 5_____ as Mr. Wang's 6_____ so he could save money and buy 7_____ and horses to give him. In that way, he could repay him what he owed and 8_____. The third man had the best plan of all! Mr. Wang was very 9_____ and said the man owed him 10_____ now.

| | |
|---|---|
| land | horse |
| nothing | more |
| reborn | reduce |
| repaid | owed |
| father | pleased |

**Now, write the sentence from the summary that contains the main idea of the story.**

_____

# Expansion Questions

**Think about the following questions, and discuss your answers with a partner.**

1. Imagine that you owe your friend $20. However, you don't have any money to repay him or her. What else could you offer to give or do for your friend instead of money? List four things. Share your answers with a partner.

| Example | I could let him use my bike for a week. |
|---------|-----------------------------------------|
|         | I could help her clean her room.        |
|         | I could give her three comic books.     |

_____

_____

_____

_____

2. In the story, two men want to come back as a horse and a cow to repay Mr. Wang. What other animals could they have suggested to Mr. Wang? Work with a partner to complete the sentences.

   a. I would come back as a _____ because I could _____.

   b. I would come back as a _____ because I could _____.

   c. I would come back as a _____ because I could _____.

   d. I would come back as a _____ because I could _____.

Now, share your ideas with the class. Which group has the most interesting ideas?

# Clapping at the Table

## Pre-Reading

**Think about the following questions, and discuss your answers with a partner.**

1. When guests come to your house, what do you offer them?
2. When you are invited to a friend's house, do you bring anything? What?
3. If you could invite anyone in the world to dinner, who would you ask? Why?

## Vocabulary Preview

**Match each underlined word with its meaning.**

1. The waiter <u>served</u> dinner. •
2. I <u>overheard</u> them talking. •
3. Your new house looks <u>marvelous</u>! •
4. The teacher <u>instructed</u> us to start the test. •
5. I was <u>annoyed</u> by the loud music. •

• a. bothered; upset
• b. to tell someone what to do
• c. to listen without the speaker knowing
• d. to give people food or drinks
• e. very good

# Clapping at the Table

Track
06

Once, there was a man named Tam who was rich but a miser. One day, Tam invited some friends to his house for dinner. As his guests were arriving, he quietly told his servant he was worried that his friends would drink too much wine. Tam instructed the servant not to serve any wine unless he clapped.

One of the guests, Li, overheard what Tam said to his servant, and he planned to play a game at dinner. During their meal, Li asked Tam how old his mother was. "She's seventy-three," answered Tam. "That's wonderful!" said Li, clapping his hands. When the servant heard this, he entered the room and poured wine for everybody.

Shortly afterward, when his glass was nearly empty, Li asked how old Tam's father was. "My father is eighty-four," Tam said quickly. "That's marvelous!" shouted Li, clapping again. The servant came into the room and again filled everyone's glass.

Tam was beginning to get a little annoyed. So when Li next asked about Tam's uncle, he said, "There's no need to worry about other people in my family. You've already had way too much of my wine!"

**Reading Time** _____ minutes _____ seconds **198 words**

# Understanding the Key Ideas

**Choose the best answer.**

1. Which sentence best describes Li?
   - a. He was very interested in Tam's family.
   - b. He was very rich.
   - c. He liked to play games.
   - d. He enjoyed drinking a lot.

2. Why did Tam refuse to answer any more questions about his family?
   - a. He didn't want to talk about his relatives.
   - b. He understood the game Li was playing.
   - c. He wanted to talk about something else.
   - d. He wanted to eat without talking.

# Reading Comprehension

**Circle T for true or F for false.**

1. Tam was a very generous friend.         T      F
2. Tam was worried that his friends would eat too much.    T      F

**Choose the best answer.**

3. How did the servant know when to serve the wine?
   - a. Tam said, "Wine, please!"
   - b. Someone rang a bell.
   - c. He heard clapping.
   - d. He could see the glasses were empty.

4. Why did Li ask about Tam's family members?
   - a. So he could find out their ages
   - b. So he would have a reason to clap
   - c. Because he really liked Tam's family
   - d. Because it was Tam's mother's birthday dinner

5. How did Li know about Tam's arrangement with the servant?
   - a. The servant told him.
   - b. Another guest told him.
   - c. He overheard Tam talking.
   - d. He overheard the servant talking.

**Choose the proverb that best fits the main idea of the story.**

6. a. It is double the pleasure to trick a trickster.
   b. Every cloud has a silver lining.
   c. In wine, there is truth.
   d. It is better to give than to receive.

# Language Focus

**Choose the best word to complete each sentence.**

annoyed
enormous
exhausted
furious
terrified

1. Camilla was _____ after studying for four hours.
2. Mikhail has been _____ of bears ever since one chased him in the woods.
3. I was amazed by his _____ house. It had eight bedrooms and five bathrooms!
4. Joann was _____ when Won Bok was late for their meeting.
5. I overheard Min say his mother was _____ because he crashed her car.

# Picture Story

**A** Number the pictures in the correct order according to the story. Then, talk about each picture.

when / heard clapping / filled all

guest asked how old /
man's mother / father

third time /
said not to worry about / family /
already / enough wine

one guest overheard /
man telling / servant

**B** What did you say? Write about each picture using the given words and phrases.

1. _____

2. _____

3. _____

4. _____

# Act Out the Story

Fill in the blanks to complete the conversation.

| a little more | arriving shortly | clap my hands | during | is very mean |
| the servant | that's wonderful | needn't worry | meal | serve any wine |

Man      Servant, I've invited some people for a 1_____. They'll be
2_____. Don't give them too much wine 3_____ the meal!

Servant    Yes, sir. When should I give them wine?

Man      Don't 4_____ until you hear my signal. I'll 5_____.

Guest     He's rich, but he 6_____! I overheard what he said to 7_____.
Tam, how old is your mother now?

Man      She's seventy-three.

Guest     8_____! *(Clapping)* Oh, yes. I'd love another glass of wine. And how
old is your father?

Man      Eighty-four!

Guest     Marvelous! *(Clapping)* Yes, please, I'll have 9_____ wine. What about
your uncle?

Man      You 10_____ how old my uncle is. You've already had enough of my wine!

Practice the conversation, changing roles within a small group.

# Summary

Fill in the blanks to complete the story.

A rich 1_____ named Tam invited some friends for dinner. Tam
2_____ the servant not to 3_____ any wine unless he
4_____. One of the guests, Li, 5_____ what Tam said
and he planned to play a 6_____. During dinner,
Li asked Tam how old his mother was. Tam said she was
seventy-three. "That's 7_____!" said Li, clapping
his hands. The servant heard this, so he entered the room
and 8_____ wine for everybody. Next, Li asked
about Tam's father and clapped again. The servant poured
more wine. Soon, Tam 9_____ what Li was doing
and 10_____ to answer any more questions.

serve     understood
poured    game
clapped    wonderful
instructed   overheard
refused    miser

Now, write the sentence from the summary that contains the main idea of the story.

_____

# Expansion Questions

**Think about the following questions, and discuss your answers with a partner.**

**1.** Write the correct word under each picture.

| glass | cup | bowl | can | bag | jar | carton | basket |
|-------|-----|------|-----|-----|-----|--------|--------|

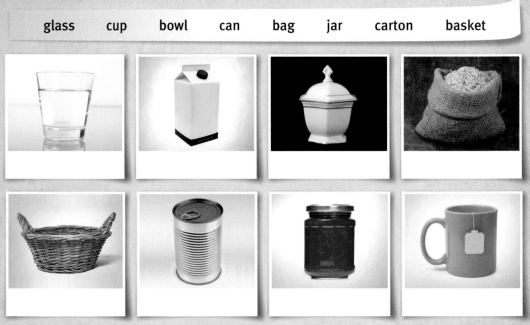

**2.** Create a game. What would you put in the containers? Choose foods from the list and fill in the blanks.

| water | cola | milk | juice | sugar | salt | rice | nuts |
|-------|------|------|-------|-------|------|------|------|
| bread | fruit | beans | tomatoes | jam | peanut butter | coffee | tea |

a. A glass of _____

b. A cup of _____

c. A bowl of _____

d. A can of _____

e. A bag of _____

f. A jar of _____

g. A carton of _____

h. A basket of _____

Then, take turns with your partner trying to guess the answers that you have chosen.

| Example | A: Do you have a glass of milk? | B: No, I don't. |
|---------|--------------------------------|-----------------|
|         | A: Do you have a glass of water? | B: Yes, I do. |

# Unit 7

# The Daughter-in-Law and the Cuckoo

## Pre-Reading

Think about the following questions, and discuss your answers with a partner.

1. Who does most of the cleaning in your house?
2. What jobs do you have at home? Washing dishes? Feeding the pets?
3. What is your favorite kind of soup?

## Vocabulary Preview

Match each underlined word with its meaning.

1. I couldn't <u>resist</u> the urge to talk. •

2. Don't eat too fast or you'll <u>choke</u>! •

3. We visit my grandmother's <u>grave</u> twice a year. •

4. The <u>cruel</u> man kicked the dog. •

5. The pirates <u>buried</u> their treasure. •

• a. to put under the ground

• b. very unkind

• c. to try not to do something

• d. to not be able to breathe because something is stuck in the throat

• e. a place where dead people are placed

47

# The Daughter-in-Law and the Cuckoo

A mother-in-law was very cruel to her daughter-in-law. She made the girl do all the housework. Despite that, she always shouted at her and told her that everything she did was wrong. The daughter-in-law was so frightened of her mother-in-law that she ate almost nothing. When she did try to eat some small bit of food, her mother-in-law would accuse her of being greedy and taking food from others in the house.

On New Year's Day, the family always ate a special rice dumpling soup called *dok guk\**. The girl put the soup on the table, and as soon as the family started eating she returned to the kitchen. The smell of the soup was so delicious that it made her mouth water, and she was so hungry that she couldn't resist tasting it. She had just put a hot dumpling into her mouth when the mother-in-law entered and shouted, "You greedy woman!" She was so surprised that she choked on the dumpling, fell over, and died.

As she was being buried, a cuckoo flew over the grave singing its sad song. The family thought the bird was saying "Dok guk! Dok guk!" and believed that the daughter-in-law had changed into a bird.

*\*dok guk: a soup made with dumplings*

**Reading Time** _____ minutes _____ seconds   218 words

# Understanding the Key Ideas

**Choose the best answer.**

**1.** How was the mother-in-law cruel to her daughter-in-law?

   a. She forced her to eat hot soup.        b. She didn't let her do any cooking.

   c. She made her do all the housework.     d. She tried to bury her.

**2.** Why did the family think that the girl had turned into a cuckoo?

   a. The bird was the same color as the girl's hair.   b. The bird flew down and sat on her grave.

   c. They thought it was saying the word for soup.   d. The bird had a dumpling in its mouth.

# Reading Comprehension

**Circle T for true or F for false.**

1. The mother-in-law was satisfied with the girl's work.     T     F

2. The girl died on New Year's Day.     T     F

**Choose the best answer.**

3. Why didn't the girl eat very much?
   a. Her mother-in-law was a bad cook.     b. Her mother-in-law accused her of greed.
   c. She didn't have time to eat.     d. She was not very hungry.

4. What did the family always eat on New Year's Day?
   a. Special hot rice     b. Cuckoo soup
   c. Rice dumpling soup     d. Dumplings with chicken

5. Why did the girl choke?
   a. She tried to eat too much.     b. She was frightened by her mother-in-law.
   c. She fell over in the kitchen.     d. A cuckoo flew into her mouth.

**Choose the proverb that best fits the main idea of the story.**

6. a. If you can't beat them, join them.
   b. If you lie down with dogs, you wake up with fleas.
   c. It takes two to argue.
   d. The hatred of those closest to us is the most violent.

# Language Focus

**Choose the best word or phrase to complete each sentence.**

1. Jed has four cats, three mice, and two birds. He _____ a horse as well.
   a. owns          b. owned          c. is owning          d. own

2. He _____ that all children should have animals to look after.
   a. believe          b. believes          c. is believing          d. to believe

3. He _____ that when he was a child, he was lonely.
   a. is remembered     b. remember          c. remembers          d. is remembering

4. He was lonely because he _____ any brothers or sisters.
   a. didn't having     b. has          c. had          d. didn't have

# Picture Story

**A** Number the pictures in the correct order according to the story. Then, talk about each picture.

a

tried to swallow dumpling/
but / choked / died

b

when / being buried /
cuckoo flew / grave

c

mother-in-law opened /
saw girl / dumpling / mouth

d

mother-in-law accused / eating
everything / in house

**B** What did you say? Write about each picture using the given words and phrases.

1. _____

2. _____

3. _____

4. _____

# Act Out the Story

**Fill in the blanks to complete the conversation.**

| a pigsty | can't resist | do much housework | has become | lazy |
|---|---|---|---|---|
| in your mouth | the smell | the soup ready | to have | hungry |

**Mother-in-law**    This kitchen is so dirty. It is like 1_____! Clean it!

**Daughter-in-law**    But I've just cleaned it!

**Mother-in-law**    Well, clean it again! Why are you so 2_____? You don't
3_____. Is 4_____ yet? We're 5_____.

**Daughter-in-law**    I'll bring it to the table now. (*A little later, alone*) I'm so hungry, and
6_____ of that soup is delicious. I want 7_____
some. Just one *dok guk*. Ow! It's hot, but it tastes so good!

**Mother-in-law**    I knew it!  You're eating again! You 8_____ food, can you?
And you've got so much 9_____ that you can't swallow it!
(*Later at the grave, they hear. "Dok guk! Dok guk!"*)
Oh.... Look at the cuckoo in the tree! The girl 10_____ a bird!

💬 **Practice the conversation, changing roles with a partner.**

# Summary

**Fill in the blanks to complete the story.**

A cruel mother-in-law made her daughter-in-law
1_____. She also said that whatever her daughter-
in-law did 2_____. Although the daughter-in-law
3_____, the mother-in-law accused her of
4_____ in the house. On New Year's Day, the girl
made the special 5_____. She was so hungry that
6_____ having some. She put a *dok guk* into her
mouth. It 7_____. As she did that, her mother-in-law
came into the kitchen and caught her. The girl was so
frightened, and the *dok guk*  was so big and hot that
8_____ it. She choked on it and died. When she
9_____, a cuckoo flew over her grave. The family
believed that the girl had 10_____.

ate almost nothing
changed into a bird
do all the housework
eating all the food
New Year's Day soup
she couldn't resist
she couldn't swallow
was being buried
was very hot
was wrong

**Now, write the sentence from the summary that contains the main idea of the story.**

_____

# Expansion Questions

Think about the following questions, and discuss your answers with a partner.

1. What do you see in the picture?

   _____

2. Do you think this family is more or less happy than the family in the story?

   _____

3. When do you think it is? Is this a special time?

   _____

4. What special food is the family eating?

   _____

5. What do you eat on your special day?

   _____

# Three in the Morning and Four in the Evening

## Pre-Reading

**Think about the following questions, and discuss your answers with a partner.**

1. Do you have any pets? What are they?
2. How do you feel about your pets?
3. Do you give your pets any special treats? Give some examples.

## Vocabulary Preview

**Match each underlined word or phrase with its meaning.**

1. I will <u>consider</u> going early tomorrow.  •
2. The doctor said he should <u>cut down on</u> junk food.  •
3. David <u>grumbled</u> about taking out the trash.  •
4. The children <u>grinned</u> at the funny clown.  •
5. Let's <u>pretend</u> that we are pirates.  •

• a. to act like something is true
• b. to complain
• c. to make a big smile
• d. to think about
• e. to decrease

Once, there was a man named Wuhan who had pet monkeys. He loved his monkeys very much and felt like they were his friends. He spent so much time with them that he even pretended he could talk to them and understand them.

Every day, Wuhan gave each monkey three bananas in the morning and four in the evening. Soon, Wuhan's wife began to grumble. "You spend too much money on those silly monkeys. There is not enough to buy food for your own children! You have to cut down on bananas!"

Wuhan was worried his monkeys would complain about getting less to eat. He didn't want to upset his little friends, but he promised his wife that he would consider what she said. He went outside to see his pets. When he came back into the house, he was grinning.

"I've talked with my monkeys," Wuhan said. "When I explained that they had to have fewer bananas, they were very upset. But then they gave me an idea to fix the problem."

"And what is it?" asked his wife.

"My monkeys said they would agree to just three bananas in the morning, one in the afternoon, and three in the evening!"

**Reading Time** _____ minutes _____ seconds   207 words

# Understanding the Key Ideas

**Choose the best answer.**

1. What is the story about?
   a. A man who ate a lot of bananas
   b. A man with a lot of pets
   c. A man who did not want to change
   d. A man who had many friends

2. Who thought of the idea to fix the problem?
   a. The monkeys
   b. Wuhan's wife
   c. Wuhan's children
   d. Wuhan

# Reading Comprehension

**Circle T for true or F for false.**

1. Wuhan spent a lot of time with his family.     T     F
2. The monkeys got a lot of bananas every day.     T     F

**Choose the best answer.**

3. What was Wuhan's wife grumbling about?
   a. He had too many monkeys.          b. He ate too much food.
   c. He didn't understand the pets.     d. He bought too many bananas.

4. Why was Wuhan worried?
   a. He didn't want his monkeys to be upset.     b. There wasn't enough money for food.
   c. He didn't want to spend time cooking.     d. He didn't want to cut down on monkeys.

5. What was Wuhan's plan?
   a. To do what his wife asked          b. To keep everything the same
   c. To give his monkeys more food      d. To learn more about his pets

**Choose the proverb that best fits the main idea of the story.**

6. a. Don't bite off more than you can chew.
   b. It's hard to teach an old dog new tricks.
   c. There's plenty of fish in the sea.
   d. Don't look a gift horse in the mouth.

# Language Focus

**Choose the correct word.**

1. There is (less / fewer) noise in the library than at home.

2. I am trying to eat (less / fewer) donuts so I can lose weight.

3. Tim moved from Colorado to Florida because there is (less / fewer) snow there.

4. Mindy had (less / fewer) mistakes on her test than her classmates.

# Picture Story

**A** Number the pictures in the correct order according to the story. Then, talk about each picture.

explained / had to /
fewer / very upset

he said / monkeys /
gave / idea / problem

loved / very much /
felt like / his friends

there was / not enough /
buy food / children

**B** What did you say? Write about each picture using the given words and phrases.

1. _____

2. _____

3. _____

4. _____

# Act Out the Story

Fill in the blanks to complete the conversation.

| in the evening | an idea | very upset | I understand what | complain about |
| spending more | cut down | monkeys | they're my friends | to consider |

Man        I'm going to feed the 1_____. I really loved my monkeys. I feel like
           2_____. I'm sure 3_____ they're saying and they
           understand me.

Wife       You're 4_____ time and money on them than on your own children!
           You have to 5_____ on their food.

Man        I don't think my monkeys will like it, but I'll ask them 6_____ eating
           a bit less.

Wife       (Later) Well? Did your monkey friends 7_____ getting less food?

Man        Yes, they were 8_____ when I told them that I can't give them three
           bananas in the morning and four in the evening anymore, but they came up
           with 9_____ to solve the problem.

Wife       What is it then?

Man        They agreed to cut down to three bananas in the morning, one in the afternoon,
           and three 10_____.

Practice the conversation, changing roles with a partner.

# Summary

Fill in the blanks to complete the story.

A man named Wuhan had 1_____ monkeys. He loved them and even
2_____ he could talk to them. Every day, Wuhan gave each monkey three
bananas in the morning and four in the 3_____. His wife
began to 4_____. "There is not enough money
to 5_____ food for your family! You have to
6_____ bananas!" Wuhan 7_____
what she said and went outside to see his pets. When he
came back, he said his monkeys had an 8_____
to fix the problem. They would 9_____ to just
three bananas in the morning, 10_____ in the
afternoon, and three in the evening.

| one | idea |
| considered | buy |
| agree | evening |
| pretended | pet |
| grumble | cut down on |

Now, write the sentence from the summary that contains the main idea of the story.

_____

**Look at the pictures. Think about the following questions, and discuss your answers with a partner.**

1. What are the names of the primates? The first and last letters of each one are given. Use the other letters to complete the words.

b _ _ _ _ n

o, b, o, a

g _ _ _ _ _ a

i, l, r, o, l

c _ _ _ _ _ _ _ _ e

z, m, i, n, a, p, h, e

r _ _ _ _ s

s, e, u, h

h _ _ _ n

a, m, u

o _ _ _ _ _ _ _ n

g, t, u, a, r, a, n

2. Do any of these animals live in your country? Which ones?

_____

3. Can you guess what parts of the world primates live in?

_____

# Unit 9 — Oranges and Tangerines

## Pre-Reading

**Think about the following questions, and discuss your answers with a partner.**

1. What part of your country is your family from (north, south, east, etc.)?
2. How do people in different parts of your country behave differently?
3. What other country is similar to your country? In what way?

## Vocabulary Preview

**Match each underlined word or phrase with its meaning.**

1. The <u>grand</u> ballroom is beautiful. •      • a. to laugh at unkindly

2. The factory <u>produces</u> cars. •      • b. dirt that plants grow in

3. He <u>bound</u> the small tree to the pole to •      • c. to tie together
help it grow tall.

4. Plants need good <u>soil</u> in order to live. •      • d. very large

5. They <u>made fun of</u> the new boy at school. •      • e. to make

# Oranges and Tangerines

Yan was an important official in a small country. The king of a nearby country invited Yan to a grand dinner. The king thought that he was smarter than Yan and that his country was better than Yan's country. He wanted to make fun of Yan in front of the other dinner guests. He told one of his guards to bring a man to the dinner and pretend that he was a thief from Yan's country.

When dinner started, the guard came into the dining hall leading someone whose hands were bound. "Who is this man?" the king asked, acting upset. "He is a thief from Yan's country," replied the guard.

The king asked Yan if people in his country were all good at stealing. Yan replied immediately. "Trees growing south of the river in my country produce oranges. But the same trees north of the river produce tangerines. The trees look alike, but the fruits are different. Why? Because the weather and the soil differ on each side of the river! My countrymen are honest. But when they come here, they begin to steal. It seems that your country produces thieves."

The king laughed. "Yan, you are too clever for me!" he said.

**Reading Time** _____ minutes _____ seconds   209 words

# Understanding the Key Ideas

**Choose the best answer.**

1. What is the story about?
   a. A clever official
   b. A foolish thief
   c. An official who was a thief
   d. A king who grew oranges

2. Why did Yan talk about the fruit trees?
   a. To show that the weather was better in his country
   b. To show that a country could change people
   c. To show that he liked oranges better than tangerines
   d. To show that people could grow different fruits on the river

# Reading Comprehension

**Circle T for true or F for false.**

1. The king invited Yan to a big dinner.　　T　　F

2. The king respected Yan and his country.　　T　　F

**Choose the best answer.**

3. Why did the king want to make fun of Yan?
   a. Because Yan was a thief
   b. Because the king thought Yan was foolish
   c. Because Yan was not important
   d. Because the king was his good friend

4. Who was the man whose hands were tied?
   a. A man from Yan's country
   b. A thief from Yan's country
   c. A man from the king's country
   d. A thief from the king's country

5. What did Yan think about his countrymen?
   a. They were clever.
   b. They were honest.
   c. They were good farmers.
   d. They were good actors.

**Choose the proverb that best fits the main idea of the story.**

6. a. If life gives you lemons, make lemonade.
   b. Fight fire with fire.
   c. One rotten apple spoils the whole barrel.
   d. What goes up must come down.

# Language Focus

**Write the synonym (word or phrase with the same meaning) of the underlined word or phrase next to the sentence.**

| official | better than | dirt | acting like |
| --- | --- | --- | --- |

1. This <u>soil</u> is very good for growing potatoes. _____

2. The <u>government worker</u> rode in a big black car. _____

3. The little girl was <u>pretending to be</u> a princess. _____

4. I think my cell phone is <u>superior to</u> yours. _____

# Picture Story

**A** Number the pictures in the correct order according to the story. Then, talk about each picture.

king asked / why / hands / tied

king then knew / Yan / more clever / he was

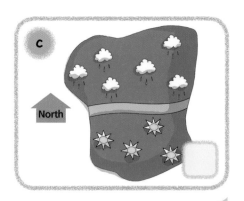

Yan / weather / soil / different / north / south

people / only / thieves when / came / king's country

**B** What did you say? Write about each picture using the given words and phrases.

1. _____

2. _____

3. _____

4. _____

# Act Out the Story

**Fill in the blanks to complete the conversation.**

| your country | differ on each side | do you suggest | hands are tied | produce |
| just passed by | on the north side | a very clever man | your people | dinner |

King      I've invited Yan to 1_____, and I want to make fun of him. What
          2_____ I do?

Officer   I'll bring in a man whose 3_____. You can ask who the man is, and I'll
          say that he is a thief from Yan's country.

Yan       *(Later)* Thank you for inviting me. Oh, who is the man who has 4_____?

King      He's a thief from your country. I believe 5_____ like to be thieves.

Yan       In my country, trees that grow south of the river 6_____ oranges.
          But the trees 7_____ produce tangerines. They look alike, but they are
          actually very different.

King      Why is that?

Yan       Because the weather and soil 8_____ of the river. People in my country
          only become thieves when they come here. Maybe 9_____ is good for
          thieves.

King      Ha! Ha! Yan, you are 10_____!

💬 **Practice the conversation, changing roles within a small group.**

# Summary

**Fill in the blanks to complete the story.**

A king 1_____ an official named Yan of a nearby country to dinner. The king
wanted to 2_____ Yan in front of the other guests. He told his
3_____ to bring a man to the dinner and 4_____ that
he was a 5_____ from Yan's country. The king
then asked Yan if people in his country were all
6_____ at stealing. Yan replied, "The same tree
can grow oranges or 7_____ because the weather
and the 8_____ differ on each side of the river. My
countrymen are 9_____. But when they come here,
they begin to steal. It seems that your country
10_____ thieves."

| thief | produces |
| tangerines | honest |
| guard | soil |
| good | pretend |
| make fun of | invited |

**Now, write the sentence from the summary that contains the main idea of the story.**

_____

_____

# Expansion Questions

**Think about the following questions, and discuss your answers with a partner.**

1. Imagine you are having a dinner party. Who would you invite?

   _____

2. Where would be a good place to have a dinner party?

   _____

3. What kind of food would you serve at your dinner party?

   _____

4. What other things can you do to help your guests have a fun time?

   _____

   _____

   _____

# Unit 10

# Lady White and Lady Yellow

## Pre-Reading

**Think about the following questions, and discuss your answers with a partner.**

1. What is your favorite flower? Why do you like it?
2. What color of flower do you think is the most beautiful?
3. Have you ever given flowers to someone? Who?

## Vocabulary Preview

**Match each underlined word or phrase with its meaning.**

1. She is <u>content</u> with everything just as it is. •
2. I got a <u>perfect</u> score on the test! •
3. The king's <u>palace</u> is huge. •
4. We walked home <u>side by side</u>. •
5. What a <u>lovely</u> poem! •

- • a. without mistakes
- • b. next to each other
- • c. beautiful
- • d. happy; not wanting more
- • e. the home of a king and queen

In a green field, two flowers grew side by side. One was called Lady Yellow and the other was called Lady White. One day, a gardener walked by. "I need a flower to start my garden," he said. Lady White replied that she was content there with her sister. However, Lady Yellow said, "Take me! I am too beautiful to stay in this ugly field. I should be in a garden."

The gardener took Lady Yellow and replanted her. She soon forgot all about her sister. Lady White was very sad and lonely without Lady Yellow. One day, the servant of a queen was walking by. He saw Lady White and was amazed at how beautiful she looked all alone in the green field. "You are so lovely. I must take you to my queen!" he said.

Soon, she was at the palace. "She is perfect," said the queen when she saw her. Everybody agreed. Artists came to paint her. Her picture was on the queen's clothes and walls. What about Lady Yellow? Well, the gardener brought more flowers to the garden, each one bigger and more beautiful than Lady Yellow. Soon, he forgot her because she was hidden among all the other flowers.

**Reading Time** _____ minutes _____ seconds   209 words

# Understanding the Key Ideas

**Choose the best answer.**

1. What is the story about?
   a. Painting a beautiful picture
   b. Wanting to go somewhere else
   c. Being happy where you are
   d. Looking for perfect things

2. Why did Lady Yellow want to go with the gardener?
   a. She wanted to leave her sister.
   b. She thought she was too good to live in the wild.
   c. She wanted to meet other flowers.
   d. She thought the gardener worked for the queen.

# Reading Comprehension

**Circle T for true or F for false.**

1. The gardener took Lady Yellow to paint her picture.     T     F

2. The gardener never forgot about Lady Yellow.     T     F

**Choose the best answer.**

3. Why didn't Lady White want to go to the garden?
   a. She was waiting for the queen's servant.     b. She was happy with her life.
   c. She wanted her sister to go instead.     d. She didn't know the gardener.

4. How did Lady White end up living at the palace?
   a. She talked about her own beauty.     b. She asked the servant to go there.
   c. Someone else noticed her beauty.     d. Lady Yellow took her there.

5. Why did the gardener forget about Lady Yellow?
   a. He started a different garden somewhere else.     b. He took her back to the field.
   c. She was just one flower among many.     d. She went to live at the palace.

**Choose the proverb that best fits the main idea of the story.**

6. a. Time flies when you're having fun.
   b. Those who try to be first will be last.
   c. The pot is calling the kettle black.
   d. A chain is no stronger than its weakest link.

# Language Focus

**Choose the best word to complete the tag question.**

aren't
didn't
don't
have
were
weren't

1. You're new here, _____ you?

2. I haven't seen you before, _____ I?

3. You used to live in Europe, _____ you?

4. You weren't in London, _____ you?

5. You play tennis, _____ you?

6. Your brothers were good players, too, _____ they?

# Picture Story

**A** Number the pictures in the correct order according to the story. Then, talk about each picture.

artists painted / queen's / walls and clothes

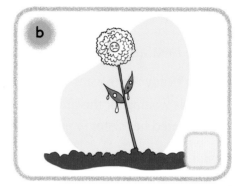

Lady White / sad / lonely / without / yellow sister

gardener / replanted / start his garden

queen's servant / amazed / alone in the field

**B** What did you say? Write about each picture using the given words and phrases.

1. _____

2. _____

3. _____

4. _____

68

# Act Out the Story

**Fill in the blanks to complete the conversation.**

| lonely | very content | my walls | ugly field | has forgotten |
|--------|-------------|----------|-----------|---------------|
| lovely | start my | artists to come | full of | take me |

**Gardener**   I need a beautiful flower to 1_____ garden. Who will come with me?

**Lady White**   No, thank you. I am 2_____ living here with my sister.

**Lady Yellow**   3_____, please! I'm so beautiful I should be in a special garden, not this old, 4_____.

**Lady White**   *(Later)* I'm so 5_____ here without my sister.

**Servant**   Wow! You are so 6_____! Let me take you to the queen!

**Queen**   She is perfect! I want 7_____ and paint her. I want her picture on 8_____ and on my clothes. I want people to see her forever.

**Lady Yellow**   (At the garden) I used to be special, but now the garden is 9_____ flowers that are more beautiful than I am. The gardener 10_____ all about me!

💬 **Practice the conversation, changing roles within a small group.**

# Summary

**Fill in the blanks to complete the story.**

Two flowers, Lady Yellow and Lady White, grew 1_____ by side in a field.
A 2_____ wanted a flower to start his garden. Lady White was
3_____ there with her sister. However, Lady Yellow said she
was 4_____ beautiful to 5_____ in the
field. Lady White was very lonely 6_____ her sister.
One day, the 7_____ of a queen saw Lady White and
took her to the palace. Everybody 8_____ that she was
lovely, and 9_____ came to paint her. Lady Yellow was
not happy for long. The gardener brought 10_____
flowers to the garden. Soon, he forgot all about her. Lady Yellow
should have been content with who she was.

| stay | more |
|------|------|
| artists | agreed |
| servant | without |
| too | content |
| gardener | side |

**Now, write the sentence from the summary that contains the main idea of the story.**

_____

# Expansion Questions

**Think about the following questions, and discuss your answers with a partner.**

**1.** Write the correct names of these flowers in the blanks.

tulip    lotus    sunflower    cherry blossom    orchid    rose

a _____

b _____

c _____

d _____

e _____

f _____

**2.** What do these flowers make you think of? A feeling? A place? A season? Fill in the blanks to complete the sentences. Then, share your answers with your partner.

| Example | **Roses remind me of love.** |
| --- | --- |

a. A lotus makes me think of _____.

b. Cherry blossoms remind me of _____.

c. Roses make me think of _____.

d. A sunflower reminds me of _____.

e. Tulips make me think of _____.

f. Orchids remind me of _____.

# Unit 11 The Cook

## Pre-Reading

**Think about the following questions, and discuss your answers with a partner.**

1. What is your favorite kind of meat or fish?
2. Some people don't eat meat. What are some reasons?
3. What is the most interesting thing that you have eaten?

## Vocabulary Preview

**Match each underlined word with its meaning.**

1. I was <u>astonished</u> when I heard the news.   •
2. The criminal was <u>executed</u> for his crimes.   •

3. Don't be so <u>selfish</u>! Share it with your sister. •
4. If you agree with me, <u>nod</u> your head.   •
5. I am <u>relieved</u> that we don't have a test today! •

•  a. very surprised

•  b. to move your head up and down to agree

•  c. not feeling worried

•  d. to punish by killing

•  e. thinking only about yourself

# The Cook

Once, a selfish emperor gave an order that nobody in his country was allowed to kill any animals for food. He wanted all the meat for himself. People could only eat vegetables and rice.

One night, a government official was astonished when some meat appeared on his table. He called his cook and demanded to know why he had cooked meat. He reminded the cook that the emperor would execute them if he found out. However, the cook explained that a tiger had killed the animal, not he. The master was relieved. Now, he could enjoy his delicious meat.

The next night, fish was served. The master again questioned the cook. The cook told his master to stop worrying because a tiger had killed the fish. The master said, "Don't be silly! Tigers don't kill fish! It was probably a larger fish that killed this one." The cook nodded and said, "Yes, I remember now. A big fish killed this small fish." The master ate with great enjoyment.

The next day when the cook prepared a duck, the master questioned him again. The cook had an answer ready: The duck had flown into a tree and died. His master just smiled.

ANY PERSON FOUND KILLING ANY FISH, BIRDS, OR ANIMALS WILL BE EXECUTED.

BY ORDER; The King

**Reading Time** _____ minutes _____ seconds   204 words

# Understanding the Key Ideas

**Choose the best answer.**

1. What is the story about?
   a. Doing only what people tell you
   b. Finding ways to get what you want
   c. Eating only vegetables and rice
   d. Learning how to find dead animals

2. Why did the master eat the animals that his cook prepared, despite the emperor's order?
   a. The cook had killed the animals.
   b. The emperor had changed the law.
   c. He was told that they were not killed by people.
   d. There was nothing else to eat.

# Reading Comprehension

**Circle T for true or F for false.**

1. The emperor wanted good things for his people.      T      F
2. The people could only eat vegetables and rice.      T      F

**Choose the best answer.**

3. What would happen if the emperor heard that people were killing animals?
   a. They would go to jail.                    b. They would have to pay a lot of money.
   c. They would have to leave the country.     d. They would be executed.

4. Who probably caught the fish?
   a. A tiger                                   b. The cook
   c. The master                                d. The emperor

5. Why did the cook tell the story about the duck hitting a tree?
   a. That is what really happened to the duck.     b. He liked to tell stories.
   c. He wanted his master to be happy.             d. He heard the story from the emperor.

**Choose the proverb that best fits the main idea of the story.**

6. a. Bad news travels fast.                    b. There's more than one way to skin a cat.
   c. It takes two to argue.                     d. A stitch in time saves nine.

# Language Focus

**Choose the best word to complete each sentence.**

1. I'm always _____ at how many people go to      (amazing / amazed)
   the movies on Saturday.

2. The movie I saw last week wasn't very _____.      (interesting / interested)

3. This week's movie was _____.      (exciting / excited)

4. It was about huge animals from another world, and      (terrifying / terrified)
   it was _____.

5. It was _____ how much noise people made.      (astonishing / astonished)

6. I was very _____ when I got home.      (tiring / tired)

# Picture Story

**A** Number the pictures in the correct order according to the story. Then, talk about each picture.

**a**

duck / flown into /
tree / fallen / died

**b**

when / prepared fish / said /
tiger / also killed / fish

**c**

why / cooked meat / emperor /
execute / told tiger killed

**d**

tigers didn't kill / but large fish /
killed smaller

**B** What did you say? Write about each picture using the given words and phrases.

1. _____

2. _____

3. _____

4. _____

# Act Out the Story

Fill in the blanks to complete the conversation.

| | | | | |
|---|---|---|---|---|
| a large tiger | all right | execute | astonished by | its balance |
| let me remind you | prepared fish | this duck | killed by | you foolish |

Master    (Angrily) Cook! I'm 1_____ you! You've given me meat! Have you forgotten? The emperor will 2_____ us.

Cook    Sir, it was 3_____ that killed the animal.

Master    Oh, good! Since a tiger killed it, I can eat it.

Master    (Later) Cook! Come here! Why have you 4_____ for me? If you've forgotten, 5_____ of the emperor's orders.

Cook    Sir, the fish was also killed by a tiger.

Master    Are 6_____? A tiger? Tigers don't kill fish! What about... a larger fish?

Cook    Yes, of course, sir. I forgot. This fish was 7_____ a larger fish.

Master    (Later) Cook! How did 8_____ die?

Cook    (Thinking) It hit a tree, but it lost 9_____, fell out of the tree, and died!

Master    Oh, good! That's 10_____ then. I shall enjoy eating it.

Practice the conversation, changing roles with a partner.

# Summary

Fill in the blanks to complete the story.

An emperor gave an order that 1_____ only vegetables and rice. One evening, a government officer was 2_____ that his cook had given him meat. He saw the cook 3_____ about the emperor's orders. The cook said a tiger had killed the animal, so the master ate the meat 4_____. Soon after, 5_____ fish for dinner. The master questioned him. The cook said that the fish 6_____ by a tiger. The master didn't think so, and after thinking 7_____, told the cook that larger fish 8_____ smaller ones. When a duck appeared on the table, the master asked what had killed it. The 9_____ that the duck had hit a tree, lost its balance, and 10_____ out of the tree.

and reminded him
astonished to find
cook explained
everybody must eat
for a minute or two
had also been killed
died when it fell
sometimes kill
the cook prepared
with enjoyment

Now, write the sentence from the summary that contains the main idea of the story.

_____

# Expansion Questions

Imagine your group is opening a restaurant. Create meals for your menu made from favorite things that your group members like to eat.

1. Circle the words that you would use to describe the meals that your restaurant will serve.

| | | | | |
|---|---|---|---|---|
| vegetarian | healthy | tasty | spicy | sweet |
| fancy | fun | unusual | fast food | fried |

2. Present your menu to the other groups.

# A Mother and Her Daughters

## Pre-Reading

**Think about the following questions, and discuss your answers with a partner.**

1. What is your father's job? What is your mother's job?
2. What do you like to do when it rains?
3. What kind of day do you like better, sunny or rainy? Why?

## Vocabulary Preview

**Match each underlined word or phrase with its meaning.**

1. We made <u>clay</u> mugs in art class. •
2. She <u>made up her mind</u> to work harder. •
3. The meal was great, <u>apart from</u> the bread. •
4. The farmer harvested the <u>crops</u>. •
5. He was <u>concerned</u> about falling in the lake. •

• a. not including
• b. a thick mud used to make things
• c. to decide to do something
• d. worried
• e. plants grown for food

# A Mother and Her Daughters

A mother had two daughters, who were both married. The elder daughter's husband was a farmer, and the younger one's husband was a potter. They lived far away and she missed them very much.

Since she had not seen them for a long time, she decided to go and visit them. She went to see the older daughter first. She asked if she and her husband were happy together. Her daughter said they were doing well. However, they were concerned about the weather. She wished they could have some heavy rain as their crops were getting very dry.

The mother next went to see her younger daughter, whose husband made clay flower pots. This daughter, too, said she and her husband were happy, apart from the weather. She wished they could have some hot, sunny weather so the pots could dry more quickly.

On the way home, the mother worried about her girls. How could she be pleased for them both? She then made up her mind to stop worrying about them. If it rained, she would be happy for the farmer's wife. When the weather was dry, she would be pleased for the potter's wife. In that way, she could always be happy.

**Reading Time** _____ minutes _____ seconds   204 words

# Understanding the Key Ideas

**Choose the best answer.**

1. What is the story about?
    a. Two daughters who wanted to be farmers
    b. A mother who learned how to be happy
    c. A mother who learned how to make pots
    d. Two girls who were very unhappy

2. Why was the mother worried about her daughters at first?
    a. They were not happy with their husbands.
    b. They were not doing well.
    c. They wanted opposite things.
    d. Their husbands could not find jobs.

# Reading Comprehension

**Circle T for true or F for false.**

1.  The mother saw her daughters often.      T      F

2.  The youngest daughter was not married.      T      F

**Choose the best answer.**

3.  What did the farmer's wife want?
    - a. A new cow
    - b. Some children
    - c. Some rain
    - d. A house near her mother

4.  Why did the second daughter want hot, sunny weather?
    - a. To help her garden grow
    - b. To help her husband's work
    - c. So she could dry her laundry
    - d. So she could travel comfortably

5.  Why did the mother decide not to worry anymore?
    - a. The daughters both got what they wanted.
    - b. Her daughters had no concerns.
    - c. She could be happy with both kinds of weather.
    - d. She moved closer to her daughters.

**Choose the proverb that best fits the main idea of the story.**

6.  a. When it rains, it pours.
    - b. Don't count your chickens before they hatch.
    - c. Don't worry about things you can't control.
    - d. When in Rome, do as the Romans do.

# Language Focus

**Choose the best word to complete each sentence.**

1.  I know the man (who / whose) works in the office on Peel Street.

2.  They have a dog (what / that) barks all day.

3.  They live in a house (who / which) has a beautiful garden.

4.  They have a friend (whose / which) garden is always very untidy.

# Picture Story

**A** Number the pictures in the correct order according to the story. Then, talk about each picture.

younger / said / if / dry weather /
pots might dry quicker

if / rain / be pleased for / farmers /
if / dry / be happy for / potters

older / wished / more heavy rain /
crops / very dry

as / went home / decided /
not worry / anymore

**B** What did you say? Write about each picture using the given words and phrases.

1. _____

2. _____

3. _____

4. _____

# Act Out the Story

**Fill in the blanks to complete the conversation.**

| thinking about | apart from | made up my mind | more dry weather | last year |
|---|---|---|---|---|
| nice surprise | potters | since I've seen | some heavy rain | still enjoying |

**Mother**      It's been a long time 1_____ you. I'm always 2_____ you.

**Daughter 1**  It's good to see you, Mom!

**Mother**      So, are you happy and 3_____ your farming?

**Daughter 1**  We're fine and doing very well. We sold a lot of vegetables 4_____.
But it has been very dry, and I wish we could have 5_____.

**Daughter 2**  *(Later)* Hello, Mom. This is a 6_____!

**Mother**      Are you happy and still enjoying making your flower pots?

**Daughter 2**  We're very happy, 7_____ one thing. I wish we had 8_____.

**Mother**      *(Speaking to herself)* How can I be happy for both my girls? What can I do?
Well, I've 9_____! I'm not going to worry anymore. If it rains, I'll be
happy for the farmers. When it's dry, I'll be pleased for the 10_____.
Then, I can always be happy myself.

 **Practice the conversation, changing roles within a small group.**

# Summary

**Fill in the blanks to complete the story.**

A mother decided to 1_____ her two daughters. First, she visited her older
daughter, who was 2_____ to a farmer. Her daughter said they were fine.
However, she wished they could have some 3_____ for their
dry 4_____. Next, she went to see her
5_____ daughter, whose husband was a
6_____. This daughter wished they could have some
7_____, sunny weather to 8_____ the pots.
What should the mother wish for? She made up her
9_____ to stop worrying. If it rained, she would be
happy for the farmer's wife. When it was sunny, she would be
10_____ for the potter's wife.

| happy | dry |
|---|---|
| crops | visit |
| married | potter |
| mind | rain |
| hot | younger |

**Now, write the sentence from the summary that contains the main idea of the story.**

_____

_____

# Expansion Questions

**Think about the following questions, and discuss your answers with a partner.**

**1.** Write the name of the job under the correct picture.

| tractor driver | firefighter | tea picker | sailor | painter | lawn mower |

a. _____

b. _____

c. _____

d. _____

e. _____

f. _____

**2.** What kind of weather would people in these jobs desire? Why? Complete the sentences below and compare them with your partner's.

> Example    **A cinema owner likes very hot weather because people want to go inside.**

a. A firefighter likes _____ weather because _____.

b. A lawn mower likes _____ weather because _____.

c. A painter likes _____ weather because _____.

d. A _____ likes _____ weather because _____.

# Unit 13 Sky High

## Pre-Reading

**Think about the following questions, and discuss your answers with a partner.**

1. What is the tallest building you know of? Where is it?
2. Do you like being at the top of tall buildings? Why or why not?
3. Do you or anyone you know live in a tall apartment building? What floor?

## Vocabulary Preview

**Match each underlined word with its meaning.**

1. The <u>foundation</u> of a building needs to be strong. •

 • a. to state that something is bad

2. The army <u>conquered</u> the smaller country. •

 • b. a very tall building

3. You can see the whole city from the top of the <u>tower</u>. •

 • c. crazy

4. It is <u>insane</u> to think that you can fly! •

 • d. the base of a building

5. People don't like it when others <u>criticize</u> them. •

 • e. to defeat

# Sky High

The King of Wei decided to build a tower that would reach halfway to the sky. He ordered that anyone who criticized the idea be executed. Everyone knew it was insane, but they were afraid to speak.

One day, a wise old man named Wan went to see the king. He said he had come to help.

The king laughed. What help could a weak old man give? Wan offered to make plans for the tower. The king agreed.

Wan explained that the distance from the ground to the sky was about 24,000 kilometers. So the tower was going to be 12,000 kilometers tall. The foundation for such a tall building would have to be 4,800 kilometers around. That was larger than the country of Wei! So the king would have to attack a country near them to get more land. After conquering that country, the king would need at least 100,000 workers to build the tower. They would all need to eat. There might be a problem getting enough food for them all.

When Wan finished, the king sat silently. Wan left the palace and, from that time on, nothing more about the tower was heard again.

**Reading Time** _____ minutes _____ seconds   203 words

# Understanding the Key Ideas

**Choose the best answer.**

1. What is this story about?
   a. A clever king
   b. A silly old man
   c. A foolish plan
   d. A difficult job

2. What was Wan's true purpose for coming to the king?
   a. He wanted to help build the tower.
   b. He wanted to change the king's mind.
   c. He wanted to help the king find workers.
   d. He wanted to fight in the army.

# Reading Comprehension

**Circle T for true or F for false.**

1. The king wanted to build a wall halfway around Wei.        T        F
2. The king asked Wan to come to the palace.        T        F

**Choose the best answer.**

3. Why didn't anyone criticize the king's plan?
   a. Most people agreed with it.        b. They didn't want to fight another country.
   c. They didn't want to be executed.        d. They didn't understand the plan.

4. Why would the king need to conquer a nearby country?
   a. To get enough people to build the tower    b. To get enough bricks to build the tower
   c. To get enough land to build the tower    d. To get enough money to build the tower

5. Why did the king decide not to build the tower?
   a. Wan said the king was insane.        b. Wan showed how difficult the plan was.
   c. Wan told the king his plan was stupid.    d. Wan offered to build a palace instead.

**Choose the proverb that best fits the main idea of the story.**

6. a. Failing to plan is planning to fail.        b. It takes two to make an argument.
   c. The bigger they are, the harder they fall.  d. Every cloud has a silver lining.

# Language Focus

**Fill in the blank with the correct word.**

degrees

hour

minutes

second

1. The bus takes about 40 _____ to get to the city from my house.

2. In summer, the weather can be very hot, and often it is more than 80 _____ Fahrenheit.

3. A hummingbird can flap its wings 200 times every _____.

4. You mustn't drive faster than 50 miles an _____ on city roads.

# Picture Story

**A** Number the pictures in the correct order according to the story. Then, talk about each picture.

wanted / help /
with plans / building

said / king / need / enough food /
the thousands of workers

king asked / how /
weak old / help

said / king / have to conquer /
neighboring country

**B** What did you say? Write about each picture using the given words and phrases.

1. _____

2. _____

3. _____

4. _____

# Act Out the Story

**Fill in the blanks to complete the conversation.**

| | | | |
|---|---|---|---|
| a hundred thousand | hear anything more | a neighboring country | be quite difficult |
| halfway to | is stupid | must be at least | bigger than | plan your building | offer my help |

| | |
|---|---|
| King | I want a building that will reach 1_____ the sky. If anyone says that the plan 2_____, he will be executed. |
| Old Man Wan | Sir, I've come to 3_____. |
| King | Ha! Ha! Ha! How can a weak old man like you help me? |
| Old Man Wan | Yes, I am old and weak. But I can help you to 4_____, sir. |
| King | Plan? What plan do you mean? |
| Old Man Wan | Well, your building 5_____ 12,000 kilometers high. You'll need a foundation that is 6_____ our country. You'll have to conquer 7_____ to have enough space for the foundation. In addition, I think 8_____ workers will be needed. It might 9_____ to feed all of them. |
| King | Hmm! I'll go away and think about it. When I'm ready, I'll call you again. |
| Old Man Wan | *(Quietly to himself)* Oh, good. That means we won't 10_____ about that idea! |

💬 **Practice the conversation, changing roles with a partner.**

# Summary

**Fill in the blanks to complete the story.**

A king wanted a building reaching 1_____. If anyone said his plan was foolish, they would 2_____. An old man went to see the king and said he had come to 3_____. The 4_____ the weak old man, but he decided to hear 5_____. The old man said that if the building was going to be 12,000 kilometers high, the foundation would be bigger than 6_____. First, the king would have to 7_____ near them. When he 8_____, he was going to need 100,000 people or more 9_____. Also, these 10_____. The king was quiet after listening to the old man. After that, nobody ever heard of this huge building again.

attack a country
builders had to be fed
had beaten them
halfway to the sky
king laughed at
offer his help
their whole country
to work on the building
what he had to say
be executed

**Now, write the sentence from the summary that contains the main idea of the story.**

_____

# Expansion Questions

Think about the following questions, and discuss your answers with a partner.

1. What buildings are these?

2. Where is each building located? Match each to its city or country.

> Taipei 101    The Pyramids    The Eiffel Tower    The Petronas Towers
> The Great Wall    The Statue of Liberty    Big Ben    Burj Al Arab

China

London, England

New York, USA

Egypt

Paris, France

Kuala Lumpur, Malaysia

Taipei, Taiwan

Dubai

# The Magic Mirror

## Pre-Reading

**Think about the following questions, and discuss your answers with a partner.**

1. How many hours a day do you spend studying?
2. What is your favorite subject at school? And your least favorite?
3. Do you like to study alone or with other people? Why?

## Vocabulary Preview

**Match each underlined word or phrase with its meaning.**

1. Don't <u>give up</u> if you want to succeed.   •

2. The plane appeared but then <u>vanished</u> behind the cloud.   •

3. The boy <u>sobbed</u> when he couldn't find his mom.   •

4. We stayed for the <u>remainder</u> of the game.   •

5. She <u>glanced</u> at the picture and then looked away.   •

  • a. to cry noisily

  • b. the rest

  • c. to look quickly

  • d. to stop doing something

  • e. to disappear

**89**

# The Magic Mirror

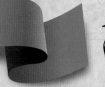 

Feng and Liu were in love, but Liu had to go to school far away. "Please give me something to help me remember you," he said to Feng. "Here is my mirror," Feng told Liu. "When you want to see me, look for me in your books."

At first, Liu studied hard. Each time he looked into the mirror, he could see Feng smiling. However, after a month, he stopped studying and went out to have a good time. The first night when he got home from a party, Liu glanced in the mirror and saw Feng looking very sad. The next night, Feng was sobbing. The night after that, she turned her back to him. Soon, Feng vanished from the mirror completely!

"That must be because I have given up studying," he said to himself. He was so ashamed that he started studying hard again. The next time he looked in the mirror, Feng had returned. He studied hard for the remainder of the year and passed his exams easily.

Looking into the mirror, he saw Feng smiling delightedly. Suddenly, he heard her voice saying, "Now, we can be happy." The next moment, she stepped out of the mirror and was standing beside him.

**Reading Time** _____ minutes _____ seconds   211 words

# Understanding the Key Ideas

**Choose the best answer.**

**1.** What is the story about?
- a. A man who wanted to please his girlfriend
- b. A man who saw a lady in a mirror
- c. A student who was the best in his class
- d. A man who wanted to forget his girlfriend

**2.** Why did Liu feel ashamed?
- a. He went to a party without Feng.
- b. He didn't pass his tests.
- c. He was not doing his best.
- d. He loved another girl.

# Reading Comprehension

**Circle T for true or F for false.**

1. Feng and Liu went to the same school.     T     F

2. Liu studied very hard at first.     T     F

**Choose the best answer.**

3. What did Feng mean when she said, "look for me in your books"?
   a. She wanted to meet Liu at the library.    b. She wanted Liu to study hard.
   c. Her picture was in the book.    d. She wanted Liu to write a story about her.

4. When Liu studied hard, what did he see in the mirror?
   a. Feng's books    b. Feng's smiling face
   c. Feng's back    d. His own smiling face

5. What did Liu learn?
   a. He could do anything he wanted.    b. His books were magic.
   c. His actions affected Feng.    d. Studying is very easy to do.

**Choose the proverb that best fits the main idea of the story.**

6. a. Love is two hearts but one mind.    b. Don't judge a book by its cover.
   c. Life is like a box of chocolates.    d. Blood is thicker than water.

# Language Focus

**Choose the correct form of the verb.**

1. This is my uncle. He (was / has been) a farmer since he was 18 years old.

2. One day, a pig (fell / has fallen) into a hole in the ground.

3. The next day, the best milk cow (didn't give / hasn't given) any milk.

4. My uncle said, "Don't worry. I (wasn't / have been) very lucky this week, but things will be better next week!"

# Picture Story

**A** Number the pictures in the correct order according to the story. Then, talk about each picture.

then / gave up / went / have / good time / unhappy

said / would give / mirror / but / look / in his books

at first / studied hard / always saw / smiling at him

when / passed / Feng stepped out of / stood beside

**B** What did you say? Write about each picture using the given words and phrases.

1. _____

2. _____

3. _____

4. _____

# Act Out the Story

**Fill in the blanks to complete the conversation.**

| ashamed of | been studying hard | delighted to | annoyed | enjoy myself |
|---|---|---|---|---|
| her back to | lovely | her mirror | saw tears | see my friends |

Feng      If you want something of mine to take with you, I'll give you my mirror.

Liu      She's gone! I'll look in 1_____! Ah! When she's happy, she is so

     2_____. *(Later)* I'm tired of studying. I'm going out to 3_____.

Friend      Liu, where have you been? I'm 4_____ see you again. But you look tired!

Liu      I have 5_____. I want to 6_____ for a while.

Friend      Great! How's your girlfriend?

Liu      Last night, I 7_____ in her eyes. And tonight, she is so 8_____

     with me that she has turned 9_____ me! I feel very 10_____

     myself. *(A year later)* I've passed my exams! Oh, she looks very happy!

Feng      *(Stepping out of the mirror)* Now, we can be happy together!

**Practice the conversation, changing roles within a small group.**

# Summary

**Fill in the blanks to complete the story.**

Liu wanted something 1_____ Feng. She gave him her mirror. She told him that he should look for her 2_____. Then, suddenly, 3_____. At first, Liu studied hard, and he saw 4_____ in the mirror. However, after a month of hard work, he decided to go out 5_____. That night, Feng was 6_____. The next night, when he got home, she had 7_____ him. He knew that she was annoyed at him for 8_____. He studied hard. Feng was smiling at him again in the mirror. After one year 9_____, he passed his exams. That night, he looked in the mirror and was surprised when Feng 10_____.

and have a good time
came out of the mirror
giving up studying
Feng smiling
in his books
in tears
of hard work
she vanished
that belonged to
turned her back to

**Now, write the sentence from the summary that contains the main idea of the story.**

_____

# Expansion Questions

**Think about the following questions, and discuss your answers with a partner.**

1. One superstition in the United States is the belief that if you break a mirror, you will have bad luck for seven years. What kind of superstitions are there in your country?

   _____

   _____

2. How many mirrors do you have in your house? What do you use them for?

   _____

   _____

3. Not all mirrors are flat. What other shapes can they be? Where would they be used?

   _____

   _____

4. What subjects do you like to study? Why?

   _____

   _____

5. What rewards are there for studying hard?

   _____

   _____

# 15 A Bad Memory

## Pre-Reading

**Think about the following questions, and discuss your answers with a partner.**

1. Who in your family is the most forgetful?
2. Is there something that you often forget?
3. What do you do to help you remember things?

## Vocabulary Preview

**Match each underlined word or phrase with its meaning.**

1. She was <u>horrified</u> to find a snake in her shoe. •        • a. to run

2. He <u>caught sight of</u> the train just in time to stop the car. •        • b. to suddenly notice

3. Her <u>memory</u> is great. She never forgets anything. •        • c. to put together for traveling

4. I have to <u>pack</u> my suitcase for my vacation. •        • d. the ability to remember

5. The horse <u>galloped</u> along the dusty road. •        • e. surprised and upset

Once, there was a man with a bad memory. Sometimes he could not remember his own name. He often forgot where he lived. He sometimes even forgot to go to sleep. His forgetfulness was getting worse. His wife was worried about him.

One day, she heard about a doctor in a nearby town who could cure forgetful people. She told her husband to go there. The next morning, the man packed a small lunch. Then, he put on his sword, got on his horse, and began his trip. At noon, he stopped by a tree for lunch. He got off his horse, stuck his sword in the tree, and sat down to eat.

Just as he was finishing his meal, he caught sight of the sword in the tree. He was horrified and thought someone wanted to kill him. When he saw his horse, he thought how lucky he was that someone had left a horse there. He jumped on the horse and galloped home. When he arrived, his wife realized what had happened and laughed at him.

But the man looked at her in amazement. "Why are you laughing at me?" he asked. "We have only just met!"

Reading Time _____ minutes _____ seconds   201 words

# Understanding the Key Ideas

**Choose the best answer.**

1. What is the story about?
   a. A man who escaped from killers
   b. A man who met a woman
   c. A man who liked to travel with his horse
   d. A man who couldn't remember things

2. Why did the wife laugh at her husband?
   a. He was riding the wrong horse.
   b. She understood what had happened.
   c. Her husband told a funny story.
   d. She knew he forgot to bring his lunch.

# Reading Comprehension

**Circle T for true or F for false.**

1. The wife told her husband to go and see a doctor.          T          F
2. The man's bad memory was cured.          T          F

**Choose the best answer.**

3. Why was the woman concerned for her husband?
   a. Someone was trying to kill him.          b. He was not eating enough.
   c. His forgetfulness was getting worse.          d. He took someone else's horse.

4. Who put the sword in the tree?
   a. Some bad men          b. The man
   c. A forgetful doctor          d. The man's wife

5. Why was the man amazed when his wife laughed at him?
   a. She had never laughed before.          b. He didn't know who she was.
   c. He felt foolish for leaving his sword.          d. He didn't remember his name.

**Choose the proverb that best fits the main idea of the story.**

6. a. The pen is mightier than the sword.
   b. What matters in life is not what happens to you, but what you remember.
   c. It takes one to know one.
   d. A rolling stone gathers no moss.

# Language Focus

**Fill in the blank with the correct word.**

always

sometimes

never

often

1. Kim goes to the gym four days a week.
   Kim _____ goes to the gym.

2. Larry eats fast food once a week.
   Larry _____ eats fast food.

3. Tina eats a banana and drinks tea every morning.
   Tina _____ eats breakfast.

4. Jim has a fear of flying.
   Jim _____ travels by airplane.

# Picture Story

**A** Number the pictures in the correct order according to the story. Then, talk about each picture.

man rode his horse / go /
see doctor / might cure him

couldn't understand why /
laughing at him / only just met

after / saw sword /
thought somebody / kill

when / stopped for lunch /
stuck his sword in

**B** What did you say? Write about each picture using the given words and phrases.

1. _____

2. _____

3. _____

4. _____

# Act Out the Story

Fill in the blanks to complete the conversation.

| and I'm hungry | bad memories | kind person | met you | might have forgotten |
| stick my sword | to cure you | wants to kill me | remind me | forgot |

**Man**   Can you 1_____ what my name is? And we live on Low Street, don't we?

**Wife**   It's Fred. We live on High Street. Did you sleep well last night?

**Man**   I'm not sure. I can't remember. I 2_____ to go to bed.

**Wife**   I've heard of a doctor who knows about people who have 3_____.
He might be able 4_____.

**Man**   *(The next day)* It is lunchtime, 5_____. I'll tie my horse to this tree and
6_____ in it as well. *(After eating)* Oh, no! Somebody's stuck a sword
in that tree! Somebody 7_____! What am I going to do?
A 8_____ has left a horse for me. I can go home.

**Wife**   Fred? Ha! Ha! I know what has happened! You 9_____ that you were
going to see the doctor!

**Man**   Who are you? Why are you laughing at me? I've never even 10_____
before!

 **Practice the conversation, changing roles with a partner.**

# Summary

Fill in the blanks to complete the story.

A man with a bad 1_____ went to see a doctor in a nearby town who could
2_____ forgetful people.  At noon, he got off his horse, 3_____
his sword in the tree, and sat down to eat lunch. As he was
finishing his meal, he caught 4_____ of the sword in
the tree. He was 5_____ and thought someone
wanted to 6_____ him. He jumped on the horse and
7_____ home. When he arrived, his wife
8_____ what had happened and 9_____ at
him. He asked her why she was laughing at him when they had
10_____ met.

| just | galloped |
| horrified | sight |
| stuck | memory |
| cure | kill |
| realized | laughed |

**Now, write the sentence from the summary that contains the main idea of the story.**

_____

# Expansion Questions

**Think about the following questions, and discuss your answers with a partner.**

1. Think about your last vacation or imagine one, and answer the questions below.

   a. Where did you go? _____

   b. Who did you go with? _____

   c. How did you get there? _____

   d. What did you do there? _____

   e. How long did you stay? _____

2. Then, work with a partner. Take turns asking the questions and sharing the answers. Don't write down your partner's answers; just listen.

3. Next, play a memory game. See if you can remember your partner's vacation. Who can remember better?

   | Example | You went to China with your family. You took the train. You ... |

# The Old Woman and the Doctor

## Pre-Reading

**Think about the following questions, and discuss your answers with a partner.**

1. How old are your grandparents?
2. Where do they live?
3. What problems do they have? With seeing, hearing, walking, or other things?

## Vocabulary Preview

**Match each underlined word with its meaning.**

1. The star athlete signed a <u>contract</u> for ten million dollars.

2. The shelves are <u>bare</u> and there's nothing to eat.

3. She <u>exclaimed</u> excitedly how great the party was.

4. I was <u>deceived</u> and lost all of my money.

5. The <u>treatment</u> for his illness was slow and painful.

- a. to trick
- b. something used for a cure
- c. a legal agreement
- d. to shout
- e. empty

# The Old Woman and the Doctor

An old lady had an eye disease which was making her go blind. A doctor said he could cure her for just $500. But if he was unsuccessful, then he would pay her $1000. She agreed and they signed a contract.

The doctor came to her house, gave her the treatment, and instructed her to go to sleep for three hours. While she was sleeping, the doctor stole everything from her house. When she woke, she was cured. However, when she came out of her bedroom, she was shocked to see that her house was completely bare!

The old woman realized that she had been deceived by the doctor, but she knew that nobody would believe her. Suddenly, she thought of a plan. She called a judge and together they went to the doctor's office.

When the old woman refused to pay him, the doctor was furious. "We signed a contract!" he exclaimed. "I cured you, so you should pay me!"

"You didn't cure me," the old lady answered. "I am worse! Before your treatment, I could see things in my house. But now, I can't see anything at all!"

Hearing this, the judge ordered the doctor to pay her.

**Reading Time** _____ minutes _____ seconds   205 words

# Understanding the Key Ideas

**Choose the best answer.**

**1.** What is the story about?
   a. A woman who broke her promise
   b. A great doctor who could cure any diseases
   c. A judge who was really a thief
   d. A woman who fought back cleverly

**2.** What was the doctor's true intention in treating the woman?
   a. To help the old woman
   b. To steal from the woman
   c. To pay the woman a lot of money
   d. To help clean the woman's house

# Reading Comprehension

**Circle T for true or F for false.**

1. The old woman was blind.                                    T        F
2. The doctor and the woman signed a contract.      T        F

**Choose the best answer.**

3. How was the doctor able to steal from the woman?
   a. The woman was blind and couldn't see.  b. He told her to go to sleep.
   c. He locked her in the bedroom.            d. He gave her sleeping pills.

4. What did the woman discover when she woke up?
   a. The judge had deceived her.              b. The treatment had failed.
   c. Her house was bare.                       d. The doctor was in her house.

5. How did the old woman win in the end?
   a. She used the contract against the doctor.  b. She found her things at the doctor's house.
   c. She stole money from the doctor.           d. She called the police.

**Choose the proverb that best fits the main idea of the story.**

6. a. Those who laugh last, laugh best.      b. Love is blind.
   c. An apple a day keeps the doctor away.   d. The early bird gets the worm.

# Language Focus

**Rewrite these sentences in the passive voice (without saying who performed the action).**

> Example   Active:  The woman and the doctor made an agreement.
>                Passive:  An agreement was made.

1. Some people warned us not to go near the fire.

   _____


2. The firemen ordered everybody to leave the burning house immediately.

   _____

# Picture Story

**A** Number the pictures in the correct order according to the story. Then, talk about each picture.

doctor / furious / when / refused / pay him

while / sleeping / stole everything / house

blindness / not cured / she / nothing at all / house

doctor said / cured / $500 / but / failed / he would / $1000

**B** What did you say? Write about each picture using the given words and phrases.

1. _____

2. _____

3. _____

4. _____

# Act Out the Story

**Fill in the blanks to complete the conversation.**

| | | | | |
|---|---|---|---|---|
| can cure | house totally bare | I am blinder | sign a contract | made an agreement |
| full of furniture | nothing at all | take everything | the disease | pay me now |

**Old Lady**  Doctor, I'm almost blind. I don't know what 1_____ is, but if you
2_____ it, I'll pay you whatever you want.

**Doctor**  I'm sure I can cure it. I'll do it for just $500; but if I fail, I'll pay you $1000. If you
agree to this, we'll 3_____.

**Old Lady**  I agree!

**Doctor**  *(Later, to himself)* Did she really think I would treat her for so little money! Before
she wakes up, I'll 4_____ she has as payment.

**Old Lady**  (Waking up) I can see clearly now. How wonderful! But why is my
5_____?

**Doctor**  You're cured, so you can 6_____.

**Old Lady**  I'm not going to pay you any money!

**Doctor**  We 7_____! You can't refuse to pay me now!

**Old Lady**  Yes, but 8_____ than before. Before the treatment, I could see that my
house was 9_____. But now I can see 10_____ in my house!

**Practice the conversation, changing roles with a partner.**

# Summary

**Fill in the blanks to complete the story.**

An old lady had an eye disease which was 1_____.
She went to see a doctor. The doctor offered 2_____
for $500, but he would pay her $1000 if he failed. They went to
a lawyer to 3_____. While the woman was asleep
after the treatment, the doctor 4_____ from her
house. When the woman woke up, her 5_____. But
she saw that her house was 6_____. The doctor was
furious when the woman 7_____. But she
8_____. She said she was 9_____. When
she had been almost blind, she could still see all the furniture in
her house. But now she 10_____ in her house.

blinder than before
blindness was cured
could see nothing at all
completely empty
to cure her
make an agreement
making her go blind
refused to pay him
was ready for him
stole everything

**Now, write the sentence from the summary that contains the main idea of the story.**

_____

# Expansion Questions

**Think about the following questions, and discuss your answers with a partner.**

1.  Why do we have eyelids?

    _____

2.  What is the job of eyebrows?

    _____

3.  Are everybody's eyes the same color?

    _____

4.  Many blind people learn to read special books written in Braille. Do you know how they read?

    _____

5.  What can blind people use to help them to safely walk along the road?

    _____

    _____

# A Boastful Man

## Pre-Reading

**Think about the following questions, and discuss your answers with a partner.**

1. Have you seen a dog do tricks? What did it do?
2. What do women usually boast about? How about men?
3. What things can you do better than your friends?

## Vocabulary Preview

**Match each underlined word or phrase with its meaning.**

1. The farmer put the chickens in the <u>coop</u>.   •

2. My uncle <u>showed up</u> last week unexpectedly. •

3. He <u>confessed</u> to the crime.   •

4. The exams are over. I can <u>relax</u> now.   •

5. The winning goal was <u>remarkable</u>!   •

  • a. to tell the truth

  • b. to stop worrying

  • c. amazing

  • d. a place where chickens are kept

  • e. to appear

# A Boastful Man

A man once boasted to his friends that he had a horse that was ten meters long and could travel 400 kilometers a day. He also told them that his hen could tell the time and that his dog could read. His friends decided to go and see these unusual animals.

When they showed up at his house the next day, the man was terrified that his friends would discover he had lied. His wife told him to relax and go hide in the chicken coop. The friends asked to see the amazing horse. The wife said she was sorry, but it was not there. The horse had escaped yesterday and run to France. Her husband was trying to catch it and he would be gone for a long time.

Next, they asked to see the remarkable hen that could tell the time. Again the wife apologized. She explained that the hen had caught an eye disease and gone blind.

Finally, they asked to see the wonderful dog that could read. The wife didn't answer immediately. Then, she began to cry. "I have to confess something." she said. "We are so poor that we had to send the dog to work as a teacher!"

**Reading Time** _____ minutes _____ seconds   205 words

# Understanding the Key Ideas

**Choose the best answer.**

1. What is the story about?
   a. A woman who helped fix her husband's problem
   b. A man who traveled to France
   c. A man who had a very smart dog
   d. A man with unusual animals

2. What word best describes the man's wife?
   a. Boastful
   b. Terrified
   c. Clever
   d. Sad

# Reading Comprehension

**Circle T for true or F for false.**

1. The man boasted that his horse could read.          T          F
2. The man invited his friends to his house.          T          F

**Choose the best answer.**

3. How did the man feel when his friends arrived at his house?
   a. Relaxed                                b. Terrified
   c. Delighted                              d. Sorry

4. What did the wife tell her husband to do?
   a. Ride the horse far away                b. Go to another city
   c. Hide from his friends                  d. Confess to his friends

5. How did the wife help her husband?
   a. She told the truth.                    b. She sent the friends away.
   c. She told more lies.                    d. She hid the dog in the chicken coop.

**Choose the proverb that best fits the main idea of the story.**

6. a. A half truth is a whole lie.          b. Let sleeping dogs lie.
   c. Even a broken clock is right twice a day.    d. If you tell one lie, you must tell one hundred.

# Language Focus

**Choose the best verb form to complete each sentence.**

1. Chang Kong Sang, better known as Jackie Chan, _____ in 1954 in Hong Kong.
   a. was born        b. is born        c. been born        d. born

2. By the middle of 1960, his father _____ to work in Australia, but Jackie stayed in Hong Kong to go to a school that taught kung fu, judo, and acting.
   a. has gone        b. had gone        c. has going        d. had been gone

3. He made his first movie in 1962. When he left school, he _____ seven movies.
   a. has made        b. was made        c. had made        d. is made

4. After 1988, his movies were more successful, and he has since _____ a millionaire.
   a. became        b. become        c. becoming        d. did become

# Picture Story

**A** Number the pictures in the correct order according to the story. Then, talk about each picture.

very poor / so / dog / got job / teacher

wife / horse / escaped / France / gone after

terrified / friends / know / had lied / go hide

apologized / hen / blind / eye disease

**B** What did you say? Write about each picture using the given words and phrases.

1. _____

2. _____

3. _____

4. _____

# Act Out the Story

**Fill in the blanks to complete the conversation.**

> unfortunately    have to confess    lied to my friends    relax    ten meters long
> they turn up    very unusual animals    when it's daybreak    follow the horse    other animals

| | |
|---|---|
| Man | My horse is 1_____ and can travel 400 kilometers a day. |
| Friend | That's marvelous! Do you have any 2_____? |
| Man | My hen knows 3_____ and can tell the time. My dog likes to read. |
| Friend | You've got 4_____. We'd like to come and see them tomorrow. |
| Man | *(Back home)* I 5_____ about our animals. They're coming tomorrow. |
| Wife | 6_____. You can hide in the chicken coop before 7_____. |
| | *(The next day)* My husband had to 8_____ to France. |
| Friend | Oh, dear. May we see the hen instead? Or the dog? |
| Wife | 9_____, the hen has gone blind from an eye disease. I'll |
| | 10_____ that we're so poor we had to get the dog to take a job as a |
| | teacher! |

 **Practice the conversation, changing roles within a small group.**

# Summary

**Fill in the blanks to complete the story.**

A man 1_____ that his horse could 2_____ 400 kilometers a day,
his hen could tell the time, and his 3_____ could read. His friends
decided to go and see these 4_____ animals. The
man was terrified that his friends would 5_____
he had lied. His wife told him to 6_____ and go
hide in the chicken coop. The wife 7_____ to the
friends that the horse had run away to France, the hen had
caught an eye 8_____ and gone blind, and they
had 9_____ the dog to work as a teacher because
they were so 10_____!

> travel    sent
> disease    explained
> poor    discover
> remarkable    boasted
> dog    relax

**Now, write the sentence from the summary that contains the main idea of the story.**

_____

# Expansion Questions

**Think about the following questions, and discuss your answers with a partner.**

**1.** Fill in the blanks with the correct place names.

The USA    Dubai    China    South America    Tibet    Africa

a. _____ has the tallest building in the world.
b. _____ has the highest mountains in the world.
c. _____ has the longest bridge in the world.
d. _____ has the biggest canyon in the world.
e. _____ has the longest river in the world.
f. _____ has the largest rainforest in the world.

**2.** Look at the pictures above. What are the biggest or tallest structures in your country? Take turns asking your partner. Can you guess them all?

| Example | **What is the tallest building in Korea?** |

# Unit 18 The Girl and the Tiger

## Pre-Reading

**Think about the following questions, and discuss your answers with a partner.**

1. What is the largest wild animal in your country?
2. Where can you see tigers? Have you seen one?
3. Have you been to a wedding? Whose?

## Vocabulary Preview

**Match each underlined word with its meaning.**

1. We <u>delayed</u> our trip until the weather improved. •
2. A <u>local</u> man told me how to find the store. •
3. He was <u>injured</u> when he fell off his bike. •
4. I need a few days to <u>recover</u> after having the flu. •
5. We ate dinner in a small <u>hut</u> on the beach. •

• a. a small, simple building
• b. to get better
• c. hurt
• d. to stop until another time
• e. of a particular place

# The Girl and the Tiger

Long ago, a government official asked a young girl to marry him. Just before the wedding, however, the man was sent to work in another town, and the marriage was delayed. When the time came for the wedding, the girl and her family traveled to the town. On the way, a huge tiger attacked them. It snatched the girl and ran into the forest.

At the same time, the official and his friend were walking in the forest. They saw a hut and stopped for a rest. Suddenly, they heard a big animal. Through the windows, they saw a tiger with a girl in its mouth. They shouted and hit the walls of the hut. The noise frightened the tiger, and it dropped the girl. She was injured, but still alive.

They took her home, but the man didn't recognize her because she was so badly hurt. The next day, a neighbor told him about a young girl who had been attacked by a tiger on her way to her wedding. Then, he realized who the girl was.

When she recovered, they were married. The local people still tell the story of the girl who was taken to her husband by a tiger.

**Reading Time** _____ minutes _____ seconds   204 words

# Understanding the Key Ideas

**Choose the best answer.**

1. What is the story about?
   a. A man and woman meeting in an amazing way
   b. A man marrying twice in a year
   c. A man and his friend stopping a tiger in the forest
   d. A girl leaving her family

2. Why didn't the man recognize the girl?
   a. They had been apart so long.
   b. She was wearing new clothes.
   c. She was badly hurt.
   d. She lived in a hut.

# Reading Comprehension

**Circle T for true or F for false.**

1. The wedding was held in the girl's town.  T  F
2. The tiger attacked the men in the hut.  T  F

**Choose the best answer.**

3. Why was the wedding delayed?
   a. The girl was missing.
   b. The man had to go away to work.
   c. The family did not like the man.
   d. There was a dangerous tiger nearby.

4. How did the man and his friend save the girl?
   a. They threw sticks at the tiger.
   b. They hit the tiger.
   c. They put the girl in the hut.
   d. They made a lot of noise.

5. When did the man recognize the girl?
   a. When he saw her in the tiger's mouth
   b. When she called his name
   c. When a neighbor told him a story
   d. When her family came to him

**Choose the proverb that best fits the main idea of the story.**

6. a. Truth is stranger than fiction.
   b. You can't have your cake and eat it, too.
   c. It's dangerous to hold a tiger by the ears.
   d. Home is where the heart is.

# Language Focus

**Choose the correct adverb to complete the sentence.**

quickly
slowly
quietly
badly

1. The big tree was _____ damaged by the storm last night.

2. There is a pretty girl _____ studying in the corner of the library.

3. Tim was late, so he _____ ate his breakfast and ran out the door.

4. The old horse _____ walked up the steep hill.

# Picture Story

**A** Number the pictures in the correct order according to the story. Then, talk about each picture.

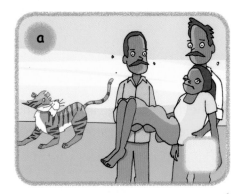

tiger dropped / injured girl / men / took / home

when / saw / girl / tiger's mouth / hit / walls loudly

tiger / suddenly appeared / carried / girl / away

when recovered / girl government worker / married

**B** What did you say? Write about each picture using the given words and phrases.

1. _____

2. _____

3. _____

4. _____

# Act Out the Story

Fill in the blanks to complete the conversation.

| another delay | be any danger | didn't recognize her | searched everywhere |
| she's injured | still alive | to shout loudly | was carried away | safe enough | rest |

**Mother**   I hope there won't be 1_____ with the wedding plans. Do you
think it's 2_____ to stop here and have something to eat?

**Father**   Oh, yes! There won't 3_____ here.
*(Sounds of screaming)*

**Mother**   Our daughter! The tiger has her in his mouth. Get her back!

**Father**   I've 4_____, but I can't find her!

**Man**   *(Later)* I like walking, but we need to find a hut where we can
5_____. Look! A tiger! It's got a girl in its mouth! We have to save
her! We have 6_____. The tiger dropped her. She moved, so
7_____ but 8_____.

**Neighbor**   Did you hear about the girl who 9_____ by the tiger? She was on
her way to marry somebody. I wonder who she was going to marry.

**Man**   She was coming to marry me! She was badly injured, and I 10_____.

💬 **Practice the conversation, changing roles within a small group.**

# Summary

Fill in the blanks to complete the story.

A girl and her family were traveling to her 1_____. On the way, a tiger
attacked and 2_____ her into the forest. At the same time, a man and his
3_____ were walking in the forest. Suddenly, they
saw a tiger with a girl in its 4_____. They made noise
to 5_____ the tiger, and it 6_____ the girl.
She was badly 7_____ and the man did not
8_____ her. The next day, a neighbor told him about a
9_____ girl who had been attacked by a tiger on her
way to her wedding. The man 10_____ realized who
the girl was. People still tell the story of the girl who was taken to
her husband by a tiger.

| young | friend |
| then | injured |
| dropped | frighten |
| recognize | mouth |
| carried | wedding |

**Now, write the sentence from the summary that contains the main idea of the story.**

_____

# Expansion Questions

**Think about the following questions, and discuss your answers with a partner.**

1. How many wedding traditions do you see? Describe them.

   _____

2. Where do you think this wedding is taking place?

   _____

3. How is this wedding different from the ones in your country?

   _____

# Racing Horses

## Pre-Reading

**Think about the following questions, and discuss your answers with a partner.**

1. Have you ever ridden a horse? When?
2. How else do people use horses?
3. Can you think of some famous movies about horses?

## Vocabulary Preview

**Match each underlined word or phrase with its meaning.**

1. In ancient times, <u>chariot</u> racing was a popular sport.

2. If we <u>cooperate</u>, we can get the job done faster.

3. I ran fast but couldn't <u>catch up</u> with the others.

4. If it's too noisy, it's hard to <u>concentrate</u>.

5. To <u>achieve</u> success, one must work hard.

a. to get what you want

b. a small, fast cart pulled by a horse

c. to give all your attention to something

d. to work together

e. to come up even or equal

# Racing Horses

**M**any years ago, a wise trainer named Wu taught the king how to ride horses and how to drive a chariot. After some time, the king started to race. But no matter how often the king raced against Wu, he could never beat him.

The king was very unsatisfied. He could not understand why he always lost. He said to Wu, "You've taught me how to ride and how to drive a chariot. But I don't think that you have taught me how to race."

"I have taught you everything that I know," replied Wu. "But you have not learned everything I've taught you. Remember, the most important thing is to pay attention to your horse. The driver of the chariot and the horse should cooperate. However, you have a problem. When you are racing, you forget about your horse. When you are behind me, you want to catch up with me. And when you are ahead of me, you are afraid that I will catch up with you. So, whether you are ahead or behind, you are only concentrating on what I am doing, not on your horse. If you want to achieve victory, you must think only of your horses."

**Reading Time** _____ minutes _____ seconds   205 words

# Understanding the Key Ideas

**Choose the best answer.**

1. What is the story about?
   a. A king who beat his trainer
   b. A king who learned about chariots
   c. A king who learned about racing
   d. A king who trained a horse

2. Why did the king always lose to Wu?
   a. He only thought about his horse.
   b. He was not trained how to drive a chariot.
   c. He was only concerned with Wu.
   d. He never got ahead of Wu.

# Reading Comprehension

**Circle T for true or F for false.**

1. The king knew everything about horses.    T    F
2. The king was afraid to race horses.    T    F

**Choose the best answer.**

3. What was Wu's job?
   a. Horse farmer                    b. Racer
   c. Chariot driver                  d. Trainer

4. Why was the king unhappy?
   a. He didn't get a chance to race horses.    b. Wu was too slow.
   c. It was too easy to win.                   d. He never won against Wu.

5. What did Wu say was the most important thing in racing?
   a. Having a fast chariot            b. Getting the fastest horse
   c. Thinking of the horse            d. Paying attention to the other racer

**Choose the proverb that best fits the main idea of the story.**

6. a. Winning is not everything.
   b. If it isn't broken, don't fix it.
   c. When it rains, it pours.
   d. Don't look a gift horse in the mouth.

# Language Focus

**Write the antonym (word or phrase with the opposite meaning) of the underlined word or phrase next to the sentence.**

achieved
concentrated
unsatisfied
defeated

1. England <u>lost to</u> Nigeria in the World Cup.    _____

2. Ted always <u>daydreamed</u> in English class.    _____

3. We <u>failed to get</u> what we aimed for.    _____

4. Mother was <u>pleased</u> with my grades.    _____

# Picture Story

**A** Number the pictures in the correct order according to the story. Then, talk about each picture.

a

if / behind / wanted /
catch up / if / ahead /
worried / Wu / catch up

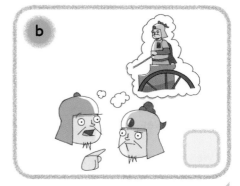

b

Wu said / king thought only /
driver / not / horse

c

although / king /
raced against Wu / always lost

d

king knew / must learn /
think only about / horse

**B** What did you say? Write about each picture using the given words and phrases.

1. _____

2. _____

3. _____

4. _____

# Act Out the Story

**Fill in the blanks to complete the conversation.**

> about racing horses   ahead of you   have to work together   I'll catch up with   much faster
> is the horse   keep on losing   order to win   race against you   drive the chariot

**King**   It doesn't matter how often I 1_____, you keep on winning. You've taught me how to 2_____. Why do I 3_____ to you?

**Wu**   Well, I've taught you all I know 4_____. But I don't think you've learned what I've tried to teach you.

**King**   What do you mean?

**Wu**   It 5_____ that you must think about. You 6_____. Then, you'll be able to drive the chariot 7_____.

**King**   So what am I doing wrong?

**Wu**   When I'm 8_____, you want to catch up with me. When you're ahead, you are worried that 9_____ you. In 10_____, you must think only of your horse.

💬 **Practice the conversation, changing roles with a partner.**

# Summary

**Fill in the blanks to complete the story.**

A man 1_____ Wu was teaching the king about 2_____ chariots. After a while, the king and Wu began 3_____. But whenever they raced, Wu 4_____. The king was not happy. He said that although Wu had 5_____ and drive a chariot, he thought Wu hadn't taught him 6_____. But Wu said that the king 7_____ he had taught him. The king could drive 8_____, but he concentrated on 9_____ with the other driver when he raced. Because he was always thinking about Wu, he wasn't thinking about the horse. The only way to win was to think 10_____.

> won
> very fast
> hadn't learned everything
> how to race
> only about the horse
> riding horses and driving
> taught him how to ride
> catching up
> to race each other
> whose name was

**Now, write the sentence from the summary that contains the main idea of the story.**

_____

# Expansion Questions

Read the descriptions, and discuss with a partner what forms of transportation are being described.

1. This has four wheels with another wheel inside, two or four doors, and a windshield. There are millions of these in the world.

   _____

2. This can carry many people. You find many of these in cities, but you can also go long distances in them.

   _____

3. This can take you quickly from one side of the world to the other. It has one or more engines. It can be quite expensive to travel on them.

   _____

4. This is very useful for carrying heavy things. Some of them have eighteen enormous wheels.

   _____

5. This has many parts joined together. It has many wheels. Many large cities have them, and some of them travel under the ground.

   _____

6. This has long flat parts that go around very fast. It can stay in the air or move up or down. It is often used to carry people who are injured.

   _____

# A Dog Helps the Police

## Pre-Reading

**Think about the following questions, and discuss your answers with a partner.**

1. How do the police use dogs?
2. What are some other ways that dogs help people?
3. Do you prefer big or small dogs? Why?

## Vocabulary Preview

**Match each underlined word or phrase with its meaning.**

1. I <u>feel sorry for</u> poor people. •

2. He lost his <u>wallet</u> when he changed clothes. •

3. The dog <u>barked</u> all night long! •

4. The criminal was <u>arrested</u> by the police. •

5. The <u>murderer</u> was sent to prison. •

• a. something people carry money in

• b. someone who kills someone else

• c. to be sad about someone or something and want to help

• d. to make the sound that a dog makes

• e. to take someone to jail

# A Dog Helps the Police

One day, a man was going home from a business trip. He had been successful and had a lot of money with him. At noon, he stopped to have lunch.

A young man, whose dog was tied to a stick, was sitting next to him. The dog looked very sad. The businessman felt sorry for it and decided to buy it. When he opened his wallet, the young man noticed all the money. He waited until the businessman left with the dog and followed him. When he had a chance, he killed the businessman and stole all his money.

The dog ran to a nearby police station. It barked and barked without stopping. At last, the policemen understood that it wanted something. The dog led them to the body of the businessman.

The dog started barking again and began to run. The policemen chased it, and the dog led them to a house nearby. There, they found the murderer. The dog ran in, jumped onto the young man, and held him on the floor until the police came in and arrested him.

Since the dog was homeless, the policemen took it in, and it became a police dog.

**Reading Time** _____ minutes _____ seconds   199 words

# Understanding the Key Ideas

**Choose the best answer.**

1. What is the story about?
   - a. A police dog
   - b. A successful man
   - c. A very bad man
   - d. A helpful animal

2. What would be the best title for this story in the news?
   - a. Police get unusual help
   - b. Homeless dog taken in by police
   - c. Police arrest a young man
   - d. Successful businessman missing

# Reading Comprehension

**Circle T for true or F for false.**

1. The businessman was traveling alone.        T        F
2. The young man was very kind.        T        F

**Choose the best answer.**

3. Why did the businessman want to buy the dog?
   - a. He wanted to give it to the police.
   - b. It was the only dog in the store.
   - c. It did not look happy.
   - d. He wanted it for his boy.

4. Why did the young man follow the businessman?
   - a. He wanted his dog back.
   - b. He wanted to steal the businessman's money.
   - c. He was going to the same place.
   - d. The businessman forgot his wallet.

5. How did the policemen find the killer's house?
   - a. They followed the footprints.
   - b. They heard a dog barking inside the house.
   - c. They chased the barking dog.
   - d. They followed the killer there.

**Choose the proverb that best fits the main idea of the story.**

6. a. You can run, but you can't hide.
   b. Two wrongs do not make a right.
   c. Money is burning a hole in my pocket.
   d. The best things in life are free.

# Language Focus

**Choose the correct form of the verb.**

1. Jane's cat usually (stayed / was staying) in the living room.

2. But last night, it (slept / was slept) by Jane's bed.

3. This morning, Jane (woke / was waking) up very late.

4. As she (got / was get) out of bed, she stepped on her cat.

# Picture Story

**A** Number the pictures in the correct order according to the story. Then, talk about each picture.

dog jumped on / man /
held him until / arrived / arrested

felt sorry for / said /
wanted / buy

ran / police station /
barked / barked

followed dog / led / to murderer

**B** What did you say? Write about each picture using the given words and phrases.

1. _____

2. _____

3. _____

4. _____

# Act Out the Story

**Fill in the blanks to complete the conversation.**

| a body | chase after him | buy him | for myself | for the murder |
|---|---|---|---|---|
| he is trying to | sad-looking | to follow him | to that stick | into the house |

**Businessman** *(Quietly to himself)* That's a very 1_____ dog. I feel sorry for him, tied 2_____. *(More loudly)* Is that your dog?

**Young Man** Yes, it is.

**Businessman** He looks like a good dog. Can I 3_____ from you?

**Young Man** Yes, if you like. *(Quietly to himself)* That man has a LOT of money! Maybe I could get some of that 4_____!

**Policeman 1** *(Later, outside a police station)* That dog has been barking and barking.

**Policeman 2** I think 5_____ tell us something. Look! He is running back and forth! He wants us 6_____.

**Policeman 1** Look! There is 7_____ in the woods! A man's body!

**Policeman 2** *(Sound of dog barking)* We'll 8_____ again. He has gone 9_____. *(To the young man)* We've found a body nearby. You are being arrested 10_____ of the businessman. *(To the other policeman)* Now, we have a new police dog!

💬 **Practice the conversation, changing roles within a small group.**

# Summary

**Fill in the blanks to complete the story.**

One day, a businessman stopped to have 1_____ on his way home. A young man with a dog 2_____ to a stick sat next to him. The businessman felt 3_____ for it and decided to 4_____ it. When he opened his 5_____, the young man noticed all the money inside. He killed the businessman and 6_____ all his money. The dog ran to a nearby police 7_____ and barked without stopping. The policemen chased it, and the dog 8_____ them to the murderer. It jumped onto the man and held him until the police could 9_____ him. The 10_____ dog became a police dog.

| wallet | lunch |
|---|---|
| buy | tied |
| sorry | station |
| led | homeless |
| arrest | stole |

**Now, write the sentence from the summary that contains the main idea of the story.**

_____

_____

# Expansion Questions

**Think about the following questions, and discuss your answers with a partner.**

**1.** Match the dog to the description of its job.

| rescue dog | pet | hunting dog | sled dog | guard dog | guide dog |

a. A _____ protects a home or business from strangers.

b. A _____ helps its owner find birds and other animals.

c. A _____ looks for people who are in trouble.

d. A _____ works with a team to win winter races.

e. A _____ is a dog that lives with a family inside a house.

f. A _____ helps blind people to walk around safely.

**2.** Look at these dogs. Which dogs do you think would fit the jobs above? Why?
Take turns telling your partner.

> **Example**   **I think this dog would be a good police dog, because it looks very clever / it can jump high / it has big ears …**

# Compass Reading Series

## Reading Challenge, Second Edition 1–3

## Reading Discovery 1–3

## Reading Wise 1–3

## Reading Time 1–3

## Compass Reading Series

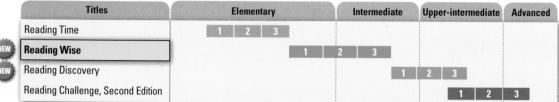

| Titles | Elementary | | | Intermediate | Upper-intermediate | Advanced |
|---|---|---|---|---|---|---|
| Reading Time | 1 2 3 | | | | | |
| **Reading Wise** | | 1 | 2 3 | | | |
| Reading Discovery | | | | | 1 2 3 | |
| Reading Challenge, Second Edition | | | | | | 1 2 3 |